PRAISE FOR UNLEARNING MASCULI|

"The book that finally makes sense of why achievement and fulfilment aren't the same thing. If you are a man who feels out of balance, I'd strongly recommend this book. It might just change how you think and therefore how you live".
Jake Humphrey, Host of High Performance / TV Presenter / Entrepreneur / Investor

"If you're finding yourself in a place where success hasn't delivered quite what you hoped and are struggling to understand why – this is the book for you."
Simon Thomas, Sky Sports, Soccer Saturday Presenter

"Cassandra Andrews' book, 'Unlearning Masculinity', is a fascinating book with many practical, insightful, useful tips, hints and techniques for helping men to actually improve their life when they reach that midpoint and they start wondering what next. Clearly, Cassandra is 'rooting for men' and this book shows how she can seriously help them. I strongly recommend it."
James Sale, Creator Motivational Maps / Author

UNLEARNING MASCULINITY

Copyright © 2025 Cassandra Andrews All rights reserved.

UNLEARNING MASCULINITY

REDEFINING SUCCESS FOR
HIGH ACHIEVING MEN OVER 40

CASSANDRA ANDREWS

Unlearning Masculinity:

Redefining Success for High Achieving Men Over 40

Copyright © 2025 Cassandra Andrews. All rights reserved.

The right of Cassandra Andrews to be identified as the author of this work has been asserted in accordance with the Copyright, Designs and Patents Act 1988.

No part of this publication may be reproduced, distributed, or transmitted in any form or by any means, including photocopying, recording, or other electronic or mechanical methods, without prior written permission from the author, except in the case of brief quotations used in critical reviews or other non-commercial uses permitted by copyright law.

Published by Cassandra Andrews

Great Britain

First edition, 2025

ISBN: 978-1-0684056-2-4

Disclaimer: This book is for informational and educational purposes only. It is not a substitute for professional psychological, medical, or legal advice. The author and publisher assume no responsibility for any actions taken based on the content of this book. Readers are encouraged to seek professional guidance where necessary.

Cover design by Kam Bains

Edited by Sophie Elletson

Typeset by Daniel Prescott-Bennett

For more resources and updates, visit www.cassandraandrews.com

For my mum – only ever a hand away.

And to you, the reader, and the special men I have known, loved, and worked with – may you find the courage to question and the strength to become the man your future self awaits.

CONTENTS

15
INTRODUCTION

25
CHAPTER ONE
HOW WE GOT HERE . . .

43
CHAPTER TWO
I'VE BEEN WAITING FOR YOU

69
CHAPTER THREE
YOU ARE NOT YOUR DAD

91
CHAPTER FOUR
I SHOULD BE ABLE TO PLAY GUITAR BY NOW

117
CHAPTER FIVE
SHOULD I SELL THE PORSCHE?

137
CHAPTER SIX
PULL YOURSELF TOGETHER, LAD

165
CHAPTER SEVEN
WHY DO I KEEP SEEING BLACK RANGE ROVERS?

183
CHAPTER EIGHT
SHOULD I BUY ANOTHER PORSCHE?

207
CHAPTER NINE
IT'S NOT ABOUT THE PENETRATION

235
CHAPTER TEN
SHIT, I THOUGHT THIS IS WHAT I WANTED

FOREWORD

To those looking on it probably looked like I had everything. I was a successful broadcaster with nearly twenty years of constant work in an industry where longevity is so hard to secure. I'd presented one of the most famous children's shows in the country during my time on Blue Peter and had now worked my way up to presenting Premier League football for Sky Sports. I was well paid and had for many, the dream job. Whether I knew it or not; I would have been classed as one of life's high achievers.

But deep down I wasn't happy. I loved what I did; but I felt stuck. Stuck in a relentless cycle of feeling not good enough to be doing what I was doing. Stuck in a never-ending battle with imposter syndrome. Everything I felt and struggled with was blunting the love and passion I had for what I did and I felt powerless to do anything about it.

To the onlooking world I had everything; but I found myself in a place where I didn't want this 'everything' anymore and like too many men; I wrestled alone, in silence. Too proud to be honest with anyone about how I really felt. The result – disaster.

Over the course of a few short weeks at the start of the 2017–18 football season, I broke and descended into a place where I was having a breakdown. Anxiety and panic attacks became a regular feature of my working life. I went from a broadcaster who backed himself to deliver; to a nervous wreck for whom just holding it together for the three hours I was on air became a monumental struggle.

Writing this foreword in 2025 I am thankfully now in a very different place. Over the past few years as I've journeyed through huge personal loss and grief, the loss of my career as I knew it, the loss of identity and long-term battles with anxiety I have learnt many lessons; but the most powerful of all is this – as men we cannot suffer in silence. We cannot allow our feelings of doubt, being stuck, empty, unfulfilled and frustrated to bubble away under the surface. We cannot carry on pushing ourselves to breaking point by pouring all of our energy into keeping it together for the outside world, whilst everything inside us is crumbling.

I wish this brilliant book by Cassandra had been around when I was struggling. It's brilliant, insightful and so practical.

If you're finding yourself in a place where success hasn't delivered quite what you hoped and are struggling to understand why – this is the book for you.

If you're struggling in silence with feelings you find hard to vocalise – this is the book for you.

If you're just feeling stuck in your life, your career – this really is the book for you.

If you're searching for practical tools to help you redefine your life and what success looks like; this book is packed with brilliantly helpful and insightful tools to help you find the life you actually want and deserve.

Simon Thomas (Sky Sports, Soccer Saturday Presenter)

ENHANCE YOUR EXPERIENCE

This isn't just a book to read - it's an invitation to reflect, pause, and unlearn.

Scan the QR code below to access free tools and additional resources to support your journey.

Because real change doesn't happen in the reading – it happens in the doing.

INTRODUCTION

'Women must hate you!' He jests, raising an eyebrow as I tell him I'm a therapeutic coach exclusively for men over 40. I'm at a networking event, the room buzzing with energy and mostly filled with men in their forties and fifties. These are the men I work with every day, high achievers who seem to have it all, yet carry a quiet, unseen weight.

The man in front of me, just 52, embodies this perfectly. Beneath the polished exterior – light blue Ralph Lauren shirt, Armani jeans and impeccably clean shoes (lessons from a father who valued appearances, perhaps) – I sense his pain. Nursing a glass of red, probably not the Châteauneuf-du-Pape he prefers, he leans in, intent on catching every word over the hum of the room.

I look at him and say, 'Most men over forty were raised to believe they must embody society's version of a "real man" – one who's emotionally strong, works hard, always wins and provides for their family. This "real man" must never show or talk about his feelings because that leaves him weak and vulnerable. So, when confronted with difficult emotions, what most men do is ignore them, bury them, pretend they don't exist.'

'Go on,' he urges, intrigued . . .

He leans in closer, so close I can smell the sharp musk of his Tom Ford cologne. For a moment, I wonder if he has social boundary issues, but his intensity suggests he's just hungry for answers. I continue. 'I believe society is responsible. We've failed to equip men with the tools to understand or process their emotions. Instead, we've handed them a rulebook that sets them up to fail. When you combine this with the pressure of deeply held values and beliefs, the impact is huge.

I see these patterns in so many of the men I work with across the UK and US; CEOs, entrepreneurs and founders of multi-million-pound businesses who outwardly seem to have it all but inwardly feel stuck, trapped or unfulfilled. Many find that having sold their business, stepped down from a CEO role, or having navigated a major life decision, they're left thinking, *What now?*

'What are their issues?' he asks.

It's a familiar look he gives me, one I've seen countless times in my coaching room, a mix of vulnerability and confusion. It says, *I didn't think anyone would really see me or care enough to listen. All I want is to be free to show up as myself, not this version that society expects.*

I pause deliberately before answering. I want him to know that I do see him, that he's not alone and that many other men feel exactly as he does. 'There are three key issues that come up again and again,' I say.

'The first is identity. Many of my clients define themselves by their achievements – business, house, car or the roles they play in society. What happens if they're taken away? What if they sell their business, get divorced, or lose what defines them? Who are they then?'

I let that sink in before continuing.

'The second is loss of purpose. My clients are high achievers, committed to winning. They've worked tirelessly to get to the top, sacrificing so much along the way, and they've done it – they've sold the business for more money than they ever dreamed of, or reached the pinnacle of their career. It's just it doesn't feel the way they thought it would. There's a hole, an emptiness. They're too young to stop working, but they have no idea what comes next.'

I can see him reflecting as I move on to the third.

'And finally, many feel trapped or stuck, often in their relationships but sometimes in other areas of life. They feel burdened by responsibility and obligation. They long to be held, to feel like their family cares about them as more than just a cash point. Then there's sex – the elephant in the room. It's often a source of frustration or disconnection, so they turn to porn, other women, or they simply shut down. They tell themselves it's fine, they'll just throw themselves into work instead.'

He's silent now, his glass empty. I can see him processing everything, the weight of my words sinking in. It's as if I've shone a light on thoughts he's kept buried for years. Vulnerable, yet curious, he finally looks at me and says, 'Perhaps we should talk.'

I've had this conversation many times before and his response doesn't surprise me.

"For decades, the spotlight's been on women, helping them redefine their roles and their worth and rightly so.

I can't help but ask, what about the men? Who's shining a light on and for them, showing them there's another way to be?"

Which is the reason you're holding this book in your hands today.

Since I was a child, I've been drawn to understanding people, especially men. For some reason, they've always opened up to me, sharing their worries and frustrations. I think back to my friend Toby, who sat cross-legged in my bedroom aged six, venting about his sister stealing his Action Man to marry her Barbie. Fast-forward to yesterday in my coaching room, where James, 52, confessed that no matter what he achieves, it never feels like enough.

I believe in the life-changing power of coaching because I've experienced it first-hand. I've been married, divorced, lost significant loved ones, faced business failures, redundancy, financial struggles, incredible loneliness and heart-break. Through coaching, I have found clarity, freedom and purpose. It's helped me heal relationships, create a business I love and most importantly find peace with my inner voice.

Today, I live a life that aligns with my vision, values and purpose. That alignment doesn't mean life is easy, but it does mean I can surrender to what it gives me, knowing it's happening for me, not to me.

One of the reasons I care so deeply about men's wellbeing is because of my stepfather, Bob. Watching him decline from advanced Alzheimer's has been incredibly painful. This cruel disease has robbed him of his cognition, speech and movement, leaving a ghost in the man I love.

Alzheimer's is influenced by genetics, lifestyle and environment, but what's struck me deeply is the growing evidence linking emotional regulation to brain health. A University of Geneva study found that holding onto negative emotions harms brain areas critical for memory and emotional processing. Research also shows that chronic stress and repressed feelings can increase inflammation in the body, a key driver of many chronic illnesses, including heart disease and dementia. Even mental health struggles like anxiety and depression are often rooted in unresolved emotional pain.

This has reinforced my mission: to help men release stored emotions, not just for their mental health, but for their overall wellbeing.

HOW TO READ THIS BOOK

This book won't change your life. *You will.*

Humans are messy, wonderful beings, each with a unique blueprint shaped by how you were raised, the experiences you've had, your values, beliefs and the story you tell yourself about who you are. That's why I don't offer a one-size-fits-all methodology to 'heal' you. Your journey to healing and growth is uniquely yours and this book is here to guide you along the way.

Each chapter gently explores key areas that have shaped the programming behind your thoughts, emotions and behaviours. Together, we'll look at why these aspects are integral to your journey of unlearning, offering insights that help you make sense of what's been holding you back. Each chapter also includes reflection points and exercises designed to encourage deep self-exploration. These moments of introspection invite you to pause, turn inward and connect with parts of yourself that may have been buried or overlooked.

I'll be honest with you: some parts of this book may be challenging. You may be asked to confront long-buried emotions, question deeply ingrained beliefs and stretch your comfort zone. If you feel triggered at any point, I encourage you to pause, breathe deeply and seek professional support if needed.

> You've picked this book up for a reason, perhaps because you already know things must change. All I ask is that you trust the process and take it one step at a time. There's no rush. Work through the chapters at your own pace, acknowledge your courage, and remember: if it wasn't messy, it wouldn't be transformational.

For this journey to have the greatest impact, I strongly recommend reading the chapters sequentially. Each chapter builds on the one before it, creating a pathway for unlearning and growth that's designed to help you create your extraordinary life step by step. That said, life is rarely straightforward, so if one chapter speaks to you more urgently than others, trust your instinct and dive in. Just know that to truly transform, you'll need to return to the beginning and work your way through.

Ultimately, how you engage with this book is up to you. You're responsible for your future and how it looks, sounds and feels. If you invest time in doing the work, you'll gain a deeper awareness of how your emotions, thoughts and behaviours shape your reality. You'll come to realise you've been living with outdated programming from childhood. Programming that's long overdue for an upgrade to version 2.0 or equivalent!

Welcome to freedom. I'm rooting for you.

CHAPTER ONE

HOW WE GOT HERE . . .

I had a professionally life-changing moment while sitting at the front of The London Palladium, captivated by a speaker on stage during their world book tour. They were discussing the importance of solitude, something I've had a complex relationship with throughout my life. As I listened intently, they shared a study by Timothy Wilson, published in Science Magazine, which found that men dislike being alone with their thoughts so much that approximately two-thirds would choose the pain of an electric shock rather than sit in their own company for just 15 minutes.

Their words were a metaphorical shock to my system. Goosebumps rose on my skin, and my heart raced as I thought about all the men in my life who I knew this applied to, men who were desperately unhappy or unfulfilled. In that instant, I knew I had to do something about it.

I met my ex-husband when I was only 18 years old . . . I'd seen him at work in Staples, the well-known office superstore, and secured a part-time job where he worked because I fancied him (or rather I fancied him in his black Levi 501s!) and thought it would be a way to get to know him.

He is a wonderful, caring man, the middle child in his family and always trying to do the 'right thing' to be seen and heard by his father. Over the 18 years of our relationship, he did everything he could to avoid and numb his deep internal pain, seeking relief in alcohol, food and exercise the way so many of us do, but none of it worked.

I am incredibly grateful to my ex-husband for sharing so much of his life with me. Whilst I was too emotionally involved at the time to fully understand, I now see that our time together was a gift, one that has given me the insight to support other men in meaningful ways.

In fact, many of the men I've loved as friends or in intimate relationships have had one thing in common: an overwhelming need to talk, to unburden themselves. Somehow, I've always offered them that space and in that moment at the Palladium, I knew deeply that this was my calling.

On the train home that evening, I spent hours researching 'the state of men', writing down ideas for a new client coaching journey. When I got home, I announced to my boyfriend, who, in his forties, was definitely one of the people who would rather take the electric shock, that I was pivoting my successful coaching and training business to focus on high-achieving men aged 40 to 60. He looked at me with a knowing smile. He'd seen me evolve over the past couple of years, each step bringing me closer to what I truly wanted to do with my life. But this time, I felt a certainty I hadn't felt before; this was the work I was meant to do.

THE STATE OF MEN'S EMOTIONAL HEALTH

I'm not an anthropologist, so you won't find this book full of expert details on the evolution of men through history. Nor am I here to start a political debate about men and women in society. What I am deeply passionate about is the emotional health of men over 40.

This isn't a random demographic. My focus comes from a profoundly personal place. I have been deeply impacted by men I love and care about who were in their forties and fifties. Men who carried emotional pain so silently it was almost invisible, yet so heavy it shaped their lives. Watching their struggles, their attempts to cope and, in some cases, their inability to express what they were truly feeling has left an indelible mark on me.

Men of this generation have been conditioned in ways I believe differ significantly from those under 40. They grew up in a world where vulnerability wasn't an option, where the unspoken rule was to tough it out, provide, succeed and suppress.

> "Emotional resilience was never taught or even encouraged. Instead, men were handed a blueprint of masculinity that prioritised strength, responsibility and control, at the expense of their emotional wellbeing."

When we look closely at the lives of these men, a concerning pattern begins to emerge, one that too often goes unseen, or worse, dismissed. Men today are facing an emotional health crisis. For many, it feels like they're fighting this battle alone.

Recent studies highlight this crisis starkly: men in the UK, for example, are three times more likely to die by suicide than women, with the highest rates found among those aged 45 to 49. The news isn't any more positive over the pond; in the US the suicide rate among males in 2022 was approximately four times higher than that of females, according to the Centers for Disease, Control and Prevention. These figures point not to isolated cases but to a widespread silence, a silence that, for some, becomes too heavy to bear.

Many men are caught in a cycle of coping that ultimately masks their struggles rather than faces them. Research shows that alcohol dependence, for instance, is nearly twice as common in men, and many turn to other avoidance strategies to numb feelings they believe they can't express.

In my coaching room, I've worked with men who pour a whisky the moment they get home, convincing themselves it's just to 'take the edge off', but the bottle often empties faster than they'd like to admit. Others find themselves glued to their phones at night, scrolling endlessly or disappearing into a world of pornography, not for pleasure, but as a way to distract from feelings of inadequacy or fear of failure.

For some, the issue isn't about numbing but striving. I've coached men who've hit every milestone on their list, sold businesses for millions, achieved elite corporate titles, yet sit across from me asking, 'Why doesn't it feel enough?'

At the heart of this crisis is the pressure to keep up appearances, to push through without complaining and to be grateful for what you've got. So, they carry on, living in silence, feeling isolated and unable to share what they're really feeling.

If this feels familiar, know that you're not alone. These experiences don't define, rather they highlight a shared struggle that many men are quietly facing. My intention is that you find this book an invitation to move beyond the silence, to take down those walls and create the life you want.

LET ME INTRODUCE YOU TO ANDREW

Andrew, 52, is a fictional character who for the purpose of this book epitomises the thoughts and feelings of many of the men I have worked with. Throughout the book, we'll journey through parts of his life, and I'm guessing that his story could be yours or perhaps that of someone you know . . .

Raised in the Midlands, Andrew grew up with a straightforward strategy for success. His father, a practical man who worked long hours, believed in earning an honest living and 'getting on with it'. University was never a discussion; instead, his father told him to work hard and stay out of trouble and if he did that, maybe he'd be able to afford a Ford Cortina and 'a house on a nice estate'. Andrew's mother, while loving and supportive, kept the family running quietly in the background, rarely sharing her own thoughts or dreams.

By his late teens, Andrew had already met Claire, his childhood sweetheart. They shared a vision of building a life together, though at the time, it was less about dreams and more about doing what was expected: marriage, a couple of kids, and a home to call their own. Claire was always supportive, the kind of person who could bring calm to chaos, and Andrew often credited her with keeping him grounded in the early years.

Ambition drove Andrew forward. He started out working for a food manufacturer, but his entrepreneurial spirit soon led him to start his own manufacturing business. By his mid-thirties, the business was flourishing. Through grit and determination, he scaled it from local to national success and eventually, his company became a recognised name internationally. Along the way, Claire played a pivotal role, raising their two children while offering Andrew unwavering encouragement, even as the demands of his work often took him away from family life.

While Andrew was building his empire, Claire was the steady anchor at home, ensuring their children felt supported and loved. By the time the kids were grown, Andrew's success had reached its peak, and he became a respected leader in his industry. Friends envied him, colleagues admired him, and his family celebrated his achievements. On paper, Andrew had it all.

Yet beneath the surface, cracks were beginning to show. As the children grew older, Andrew couldn't shake the feeling that Claire's focus remained on them, leaving him on the sidelines. He loved her deeply, but it felt as though they had grown apart; she was devoted to the family, and he had become the provider. While she saw to the emotional needs of their children, Andrew often felt unseen and unheard in his own home. The connection they once shared felt distant, replaced by a polite companionship that left him wondering if they were still on the same team. Despite everything they had built together, he couldn't help but feel a quiet, growing sense of loneliness.

When he was 49, a lucrative buyout offer came along and after careful thought, he took it. On the day he signed the papers, friends congratulated him, his family celebrated, and people toasted to his success. Everyone expected he'd be elated, finally free to enjoy all that hard work. But as he walked out of his office that day, he felt like there was a hole. It was as though he'd just handed over part of himself he could never get back. He tried to shake the feeling, telling himself that he should be happy, that he'd 'made it'. It's just he couldn't quieten the voice in his mind that was asking, *Is this really it, is this what success feels like?*

In the years that followed, Andrew filled his days with the trappings of wealth. He bought luxury cars, travelled to exotic places, invested in businesses he thought might keep him busy. But something still gnawed at him. He'd attend dinners and events where people praised him, and for a moment, he'd feel that familiar surge of pride. But there was always an ache he couldn't quite place, a quiet emptiness.

Sometimes, he'd sit alone in his expansive kitchen in the early hours, staring at the marble countertops, the carefully selected units, scrolling through social media, seeing former colleagues still grinding away, while he sat, disconnected from any sort of purpose.

On nights like these, he'd pour himself a drink, the silence around him only amplifying the questions in his mind. *What's wrong with me? Why doesn't any of this feel like enough?*

His family sensed it, too. Claire would ask him if he was all right, a touch of worry in her voice, but he'd shrug it off, giving her the same easy answer: 'Just thinking about what's next.' His children, both grown and independent, would call now and then, asking for advice, but he'd often end the calls feeling like an imposter, unsure if the wisdom he offered matched the doubt and restlessness he carried within.

There were fleeting moments when he thought about opening up, telling someone about the quiet sadness that had settled in his chest, the sense that he was drifting in his own life. However, each time, that familiar voice in his head would stop him. *You're the successful one. You're supposed to have it all together. Don't let them see your weakness.* So, he carried on, wearing the mask of the successful man, while inside, he felt more lost than ever.

Now, at 52, Andrew is exhausted. Despite the money, the freedom, the outward success, he feels trapped by an invisible weight, a responsibility to live up to an image he'd created but no longer feels is his own. What he wants, more than anything, is a life that feels real, one where he doesn't have to measure himself by what others expect or by what he owns. Most of all, he wants to be seen and heard, not as 'the successful entrepreneur', but as himself, a man in search of something that goes beyond money, beyond titles, beyond all the things he once thought would make him complete.

While Andrew's story centres on the journey of an entrepreneur, it's also the story of many CEOs, CFOs, CMOs and other high-achieving professionals. His experience is a mirror for anyone who has ever questioned whether outward success is enough to fill the deeper void within.

A 'REAL MAN'

If you're anything like many of my clients, I know you're all about the outcome and at this point probably want to dive in and get to the part where I tell you how to live your best life. I think it's important, however, to take a moment to pause briefly to consider how we got here so that you can be reassured that what you're thinking and feeling is actually very normal and you're not alone.

Traditionally, gender roles reinforced the idea that men should be strong and stoic and supress vulnerability. Indeed, most men over 40 were brought up to believe that a 'real man' embodies these traits:

- **Provides** – The idea of masculinity has long been tied to the role of a provider. A 'real man' takes on the responsibility of ensuring the financial and physical wellbeing for his loved ones. This isn't just about money; it's a deep-seated drive to protect, to create stability and to serve those who depend on him.
- **Is strong** – Strength, both physical and emotional, is often seen as the basis of masculinity. A 'real man' doesn't ask for help; he handles challenges alone and faces adversity with a stiff upper lip.
- **Always wins** – Success has traditionally been a marker of masculinity, whether it's in your career, personal accomplishments or social

status. Winning becomes a measure of worth. The desire to achieve and to be recognised fuels ambition, but it also sets an endless high bar, leaving many men feeling like they're never quite 'enough'.

For many men, these unwritten rules to being a 'real man' is clear; you must never be afraid, emotional, or soft. Tears are a sign of failure, vulnerability a sign of weakness. These ideas or beliefs may have encouraged men to be ambitious, responsible and resilient but at what cost?

Masculinity is evolving; it's time to acknowledge that it's okay to value strength and resilience whilst also creating space for vulnerability and emotional honesty. Understanding this is key to honouring the positive intentions of masculinity whilst letting go of the parts that no longer serve you.

PUTTING UP WALLS

The journey of emotions from boyhood to manhood is shaped by societal expectations, family dynamics and each man's unique experiences. In early childhood, boys experience life with curiosity and openness, exploring the world around them and expressing a full range of emotions: joy, excitement, sadness, fear. However, these natural responses often start to shift when boys hear phrases like, 'pull yourself together', 'big boys don't cry', or 'don't be such a baby'. Gradually, these words plant seeds, creating beliefs that certain emotions are wrong or weak. It's essential to recognise that fathers (and mothers) who spoke these words often did so out of love and protection; they too were raised with the same beliefs, instilled by their own parents. This isn't about blaming, it's about understanding.

As boys grow into adolescence, they begin exploring their identity, trying to work out who they are and where they fit in. Hormonal shifts and social pressure add complexity to their journey. During these years, peer relationships grow in significance and young men often find that fitting in requires conforming to social expectations about masculinity. As a result, they start to suppress emotions seen as 'unmanly', so vulnerability is hidden behind humour, anger, or silence.

By the time these boys transition into adulthood, the pattern is programmed in. Now, the expectation is to be tough, stoic and self-sufficient, even if it means internalising what they're thinking and feeling rather than seeking support. At one time, this survival mechanism – the ability to 'put up walls' – was perhaps a way to be accepted, to be strong, to avoid being different. For many men today, it has become a prison, creating a generation who are aching for connection and desperate to talk but don't feel safe enough to do so.

The challenge is that these walls are so deeply internalised, so much a part of what it means to be a man, that letting them go feels unsafe. They're scared that if they take down the walls, they'll be left exposed and vulnerable. Yet, without taking them down, the connection, fulfilment and freedom they're searching for remain out of reach.

THE IMPACT OF MASCULINITY

In response to this childhood conditioning, most men, when confronted with challenging emotions, do what they've been taught: ignore them, pretend they don't exist, or push them down. After all, that's what you're supposed to do if you're a 'real man', right?

However, repressing emotions doesn't make them disappear. In fact, it can have serious, even fatal consequences, including unhappy relationships or divorce, physical pain, addiction, dementia or suicide. Many of these topics we look at later in the book.

These consequences aren't inevitable, but they're real and I see them in my coaching room. If any of these resonate with you, know that recognising these patterns is the first step to making a change. Together, we'll begin exploring ways to open up, express and process emotions healthily, allowing you to move beyond survival and into a life that feels truly meaningful.

EVOLUTION

To really understand what modern masculinity is all about, we have to look back at where it all started. For most of human history, being a man was all about survival; think physical strength, aggression and the instinct to protect and provide for your family or tribe. These traits weren't just important; they were essential. They became ingrained in what it meant to be a 'real man'.

However, as the world has changed, so have the expectations placed upon men. The old evolutionary programming that once helped men thrive is now outdated and needs upgrading. In today's world, survival isn't about fighting or finding food; it's about creating meaningful relationships and adapting to an ever-changing social landscape.

Take Andrew, for example. He worked hard his entire life, accumulating wealth, status and possessions – a big house, a driveway full of cars, the latest gadgets. On the surface, it looked like he'd made it. But underneath, there was still this nagging need to keep proving himself, to keep up with others, or even outdo them. This drive to verify his success through external things isn't about vanity; it's deeply rooted in our evolutionary history. For our ancestors, a man's ability to gather resources and display them was a direct signal of his competence and status within the tribe. The more resources he had, the more he could provide for his family and contribute to the tribe's survival, making him a desirable mate and earning him respect and influence.

So, as you turn inwards for personal reflection and healing, it's essential to recognise that your brain carries the imprints of an ancient past. The way you react to stress, connect with others and seek fulfilment is all rooted in millions of years of evolution. Our ancestors relied on tight-knit communities for survival, which hardwired your brains to crave connection, security and belonging. These primal instincts still drive you today, often shaping your sense of self-worth based on external achievements rather than inner fulfilment.

Recognising this evolution offers us an opportunity to unlearn some of these outdated expectations and create space for new definitions of success, ones that prioritise internal peace, emotional connection and genuine fulfilment over constant external achievement. Understanding this background can be incredibly liberating; it allows us to approach our thoughts and emotions with greater compassion. Rather than seeing our struggles as personal flaws, we can recognise them as natural responses rooted in the brain's ancient design. This shift lets us move away from a relentless pursuit of validation and towards a life that feels truly aligned with who we are.

A CALL TO COMPASSION AND CURIOSITY

As we move through this book together, you may find yourself encountering beliefs and patterns you didn't even realise you were carrying – ideas about what it means to be a real or successful man. Some of these ideas might feel so ingrained that they seem intimately part of who you are. However, they are only ideas, and they can be unlearned, reprogrammed or even released.

Give yourself permission to question these beliefs gently, to examine them not as fixed truths but as rules and stories you've lived by. Some of these stories have served you well, helping you reach heights you may never have thought possible. But if they no longer bring fulfilment, it's okay to let them go.

This isn't about fixing yourself or getting it right. It's about uncovering what lies beneath the surface, letting go of what no longer serves you and reconnecting with the parts of yourself that may have been hidden away. Think of this process as an exploration, a quiet journey into yourself, where there's no rush and no right answer, only a growing awareness of who you truly are, beyond your roles, titles and achievements.

So, as you turn the page, know that this is a safe space, a place where you can be both curious and compassionate. Let go of any pressure to have it all figured out. Instead, allow yourself to explore with openness and curiosity.

You're not alone. And as we move forward together, you'll find that you have everything within you to create a life that feels truly, deeply like yours.

YOUR UNLEARNING

As we begin this journey together, let's summarise some of the ideas we explored in this chapter. These points are here to encourage you to start gently noticing things you might want to unlearn.

1. **Unlearn the belief that solitude is something to avoid.** Consider what it could feel like to truly sit with your own thoughts.
2. **Unlearn the idea that emotional strength means suppressing vulnerability.** How could strength and openness co-exist?
3. **Unlearn the belief that you always have to *win* or *achieve*.** Explore what it might mean to let go of societal expectations around success.
4. **Unlearn the habit of building walls to protect yourself from feeling.** What might it look like to begin gently taking down those walls?
5. **Unlearn the expectation that success alone brings fulfilment.** Consider Andrew's story and the emptiness he felt despite his achievements.

CHAPTER TWO

I'VE BEEN WAITING FOR YOU

Andrew used to believe his identity was about the roles he played: husband, father, business owner. For years, he wore these titles with pride, trusting that they defined his value and purpose. But over time, an unshakeable feeling crept in, a subtle ache for something missing that he couldn't quite name. He'd arrive home, share a few words with his wife and drift through his evenings feeling like a supporting actor in his own life. Despite his success, he felt bound by expectations and responsibility.

As he began to turn inwards, Andrew realised that his beliefs about himself and others were driving him in ways he'd never truly considered. He'd spent decades being 'the man' for everyone else, convinced that his happiness depended on their approval. The cost had been a quiet erosion of his own identity, his personal desires and his connection with himself.

The relationship we hold with ourselves shapes every other connection in our lives. Consider that for a moment; the way you behave, your insecurities and your beliefs all influence how you show up with your partner, your children and your team. So, if you want better relationships with others, you must begin by focusing on yourself. You must love yourself fully, even more than your family, so they can experience the very best version of you.

This notion may feel uncomfortable; after all, society has conditioned you to see self-care as selfish. Consider the overused saying that in a plane emergency, you need to secure your own oxygen mask first taking them down Reflect on where in your life you might be starved of oxygen and where a bit more self-compassion could restore your energy. If you're unsure where to start, you're not alone and this chapter is your guide.

Like any meaningful journey, it starts by understanding exactly where you are right now. In business, you wouldn't dream of launching a new product or strategy without first assessing your current position; the same applies here. Before you can create the life you truly want, you need to take stock of who and where you are at this moment in time, the beliefs driving your decisions and the patterns shaping your behaviours. Think of this chapter as your personal audit, the foundation for everything that follows.

I know it might be tempting to skim through or even skip this part. In my experience, high achievers like you are often eager to jump straight to the 'fix it' stage. However, self-awareness is the cornerstone of change, and this chapter is designed to help you uncover where you're starting from. You'll explore the roles you've played, the beliefs you've built, and the unconscious programming quietly influencing your life. By the end, you'll have clarity about where you are so you can move to the rest of the book with purpose and intention.

So, settle in, this is where it all begins; after all, the deep authentic you has been waiting for you, your whole life.

BECOMING AWARE

'Until you make the unconscious conscious, it will direct your life and you will call it fate.' Carl Jung

Are you finding yourself going through the motions of life, knowing that there's more than this hamster wheel of responsibility, or perhaps co-existing in a marriage where you're living more like brother and sister? Then perhaps you need to shine a light on the relationship you have with yourself and turn inwards; by doing so, you can live a life that's intentional, fulfilling and offers the freedom and purpose you want.

Self-awareness is the first critical step in creating your best life. It's the ability to consciously recognise your thoughts, emotions, behaviours and motivations. When you're aware, you're empowered to take ownership of your life, shifting from passive bystander to active participant in shaping your reality.

I'm here to guide you, so you can stop settling and move towards the life you want. Remember, though, awareness is the foundation. You can't let go of what you aren't conscious of, so the exercises in this chapter will help you start to understand:

- Where you may be blocked or what's holding you back.
- Potential patterns from the past that still influence your present.
- Limiting beliefs or 'rules' that might restrict your future.
- Inner conflicts where different parts of you pull in opposing directions.

"Self-awareness is the first critical step in creating your best life."

For some men, this journey is liberating, providing relief and new insights. For others, it may stir up some discomfort in the process. If you notice any feelings of discomfort or resistance as you move through these exercises, embrace them, this means you're moving forwards. Growth requires us to get comfortable with the discomfort of change.

That said, it's essential to recognise your own limits. If any of the exercises feel overwhelming, pause, seek support from a friend, or reach out to a professional. There's strength in knowing when to lean on others.

THE UNCONSCIOUS MIND

To truly deepen your self-awareness, you need to look beneath the surface, because while your conscious mind believes it's in charge, it's your unconscious mind that quietly runs the show, influencing almost 95% of what you think, feel and do. So, who's really in control of your reality?

Imagine your mind as an iceberg. What you see above the water, that's your conscious mind. It's where all the action happens that you're aware of: thinking, reasoning, making decisions and all the day-to-day things that keeps you ticking. It's the part of you that's reading this (perhaps taking notes!) and remembering to pay the bills. You could say it's like the captain of the ship, navigating and making decisions you're actively aware of. It's logical, it's deliberate and it likes to think it's in charge.

Now, dip below the surface and you hit the vast, mysterious world of the unconscious mind. It's the programming that's running quietly in the background. It stores all your deep-seated beliefs, past experiences, emotions and habits. Think of it as the autopilot of your mind, handling everything you do without thinking, like driving your car whilst lost in thought, or the emotional reaction you have to a song without knowing why.

Let's not forget the body. Your unconscious mind keeps your heart beating, your lungs breathing and even signals when you're thirsty – all without conscious thought. It's a remarkable system that keeps you alive and kicking, allowing you the opportunity to focus on enjoying life and tackling bigger conscious challenges.

By understanding both, you can start to see why you do the things you do and why certain things push your buttons – and how you can start changing deep-seated habits and beliefs. It's not about making you more efficient, it's about deepening your self-awareness by becoming aware of the fears, old wounds and long-held beliefs that reside there. Programming that was written long ago, dictating who you are and how you react to the world, often without conscious approval. So, let's get the whole iceberg working for you, not just the tip!

To create the life you want, you need to get both your conscious and unconscious mind working in harmony, which is much of the work I do with my clients. Here are a few things to be aware of regarding the unconscious mind:

- **It can't process negatives:** The unconscious mind doesn't recognise don't or not. So, if you say, 'I don't want to be stressed,' it latches onto stressed. Use this knowledge to direct it towards what you do want; for example, 'I want to feel calm.'

- **It needs direction:** Unless it's aligned with your conscious goals, the unconscious mind can follow its own path, often working against what you consciously want. You must tell your unconscious mind that you want to create real, lasting change.
- **It stores and represses memories:** The unconscious mind holds all your memories (even the ones you don't consciously remember!); however, its job is to keep us safe, so if memories are too painful to deal with, it will repress them to allow you to get on with life. Uncovering these repressed memories will help you understand some of your automatic responses.
- **It keeps us safe:** Wondering why you can't stop that self-destructive habit? Be reassured that your unconscious mind has created it to keep you safe. It might not be logical, but it will have a positive intention for doing so. Which is why I say to my clients, 'You can't solve an unconscious problem consciously.'

UNLOCKING YOUR INNER RESOURCES

Once you begin to understand the power of your unconscious mind, the next step is learning how to reprogramme it with instructions for the life you consciously want. This is why I use neuro-linguistic programming (NLP) with my clients. I've seen firsthand the transformational impact it can have, helping people rewrite the patterns holding them back.

NLP is more than just a tool; it's a way of seeing the world and yourself with fresh eyes. Have you ever felt stuck, repeating the same patterns or hearing the same voice in your head telling you what you can't do? NLP offers a way to pause that loop and rewrite the story. It helps you step back, see what's really going on beneath the surface, and understand how your thoughts, language and behaviours are all intricately connected.

What I love about NLP is its focus on curiosity. It encourages you to approach life and yourself with an open mind, challenging the assumptions and beliefs that might be holding you back. Imagine being able to shift a moment of doubt into one of possibility, transform a relationship or achieve the meaningful goals you've set for yourself.

Throughout this book, I'll weave in principles and techniques from NLP to help us uncover the programming, beliefs and values that may be running quietly in the background of your life. By shining a light on them, you'll have the power to break free from the habits and mindsets that no longer serve you. This is about stepping into the version of yourself you've always known was possible.

A foundational aspect of NLP is its presuppositions – underlying beliefs that shape our thoughts, behaviours and communication. By working with these guiding principles, you can shift your mindset towards the life you want.

One of these core presuppositions is: **YOU have all the resources inside you.**

This is the assumption that everyone has the inner resources, for example resilience, wisdom and leadership, needed to face challenges and achieve their goals. Imagine, for instance, a man of 54 who has just sold his business and feels a lack of purpose. The belief that 'individuals are resourceful' suggests that he already has the skills and wisdom within himself to find new meaning in life. By reflecting on his experiences, passions and strengths, he can explore fresh opportunities and create a fulfilling future.

This principle matters because you, too, already have all the resources within you to shape the life you desire. The key to unlocking these resources is self-awareness and asking the right questions.

YOUR EMOTIONAL TOOLKIT

As your coach on this journey, my intention is for you to feel curious and supported as you explore each chapter and consider what it means for you personally. It's important that if you feel any anxiety or discomfort, you have some practices that can help bring you back to a grounded, present state.

Yes, I get it, 'grounded' sounds like something you might hear right before someone hands you kombucha and a mantra. If that's your thing, you're probably already sold on it! But for the rest of you, stick with me.

Grounding isn't about incense or chanting; it's about pulling yourself out of the chaos in your head and planting your feet firmly in the here and now. It's a no-nonsense way to calm your nervous system, steady your breath and remind yourself that you're not, in fact, being chased by a sabre-toothed tiger.

Which is why I recommend you create an emotional toolkit – practices that can help bring you back to a grounded, present state. Even if you don't feel you need it right now, I encourage you to take a few moments to create your own toolkit in advance so it's there if you need it. Here are some suggestions for both proactive practices (to use regularly to reduce triggers) and reactive practices (to use in moments of anxiety, frustration or sadness).

- **Sensory grounding:** When you're triggered, shifting from your head into your body can help you reconnect to the present. Start with a deep breath, sigh out the exhale, and then engage your senses: notice five things you can see, four you can touch, three you can hear, two you can smell, and one you can taste.

  This exercise works by redirecting your focus from spiralling thoughts to the tangible world around you. By engaging your senses, you calm your nervous system and anchor yourself in the present moment, creating a sense of stability and control when emotions feel overwhelming.

- **Breathwork:** Intentional breathing is a powerful way to signal safety to your nervous system, helping to regulate stress responses. Techniques like 4-7-8 Breathing, Box Breathing and Alternate Nostril Breathing can be found at the end of this book or as an audio version on the resources page of my website cassandraandrews.com/unlearning

- **Journaling:** Journaling is like talking to yourself on paper; it's about getting the thoughts and emotions out of your head. By writing them down, you gain distance and perspective, something known as cognitive defusion. Our minds naturally have a negativity bias, so journaling can help clear out the catastrophising thoughts. If you're new to journaling, I offer a free guide on my website to help you get started: cassandraandrews.com/journaling.

- **Meditation:** A busy mind doesn't mean you can't meditate! Let's clear up a few myths: you don't need to sit like Buddha, have a blank mind, or meditate for hours to experience benefits. Ten to twenty minutes a day is often enough. I highly recommend *Bliss More* by Light Watkins for a simple, practical approach to meditation that can work for anyone.

OVER TO YOU . . .

LET THE AWAKENING BEGIN!

There are four tools I'd like to introduce you to, to help you start your journey of self-awareness. If you're like many of my clients, I'm sure you want to get stuck in . . . However, there's no rush, this is about connecting with yourself and your deepest desires and that might feel unfamiliar. So, I invite you to put the kettle on, move away from distractions, take a deep breath and mindfully work through the exercises. It doesn't matter what order you do them in, do what is right for you.

EXERCISE 1

THE WHEEL OF LIFE

Even the greatest achievers often feel a gap between where they are and where they truly want to be. Perhaps your career is thriving, yet your intimate relationships feel strained. Or maybe your relationships are flourishing, but your physical health or connection with your children isn't where you'd like it to be. We all have areas that call for greater focus to create or sustain the life we want.

The Wheel of Life is a powerful visual tool that helps you identify where you're in balance and where you might need more attention. To get started, download the exercise from my website cassandraandrews.com/unlearning. Once you have the worksheet, score each area of your life on a scale of 1–10 (1 being very poor,

10 outstanding) across key categories like career, family, health and personal growth. Shade in each section to create a snapshot of your life's balance.

Once you've completed your wheel, reflect on the following questions:

- **What stands out to you as you look at your wheel?**
- **If this were a real wheel, how bumpy would the journey be?**
- **Which area feels like the biggest priority for you right now, and why?**
- **What beliefs are holding you back in that area and what empowering beliefs could you adopt?**

This exercise is just the starting point on your path to greater balance and fulfilment. A deeper exploration of the Wheel of Life, along with guiding questions, is available on the downloadable handout on my website cassandraandrews.com/unlearning.

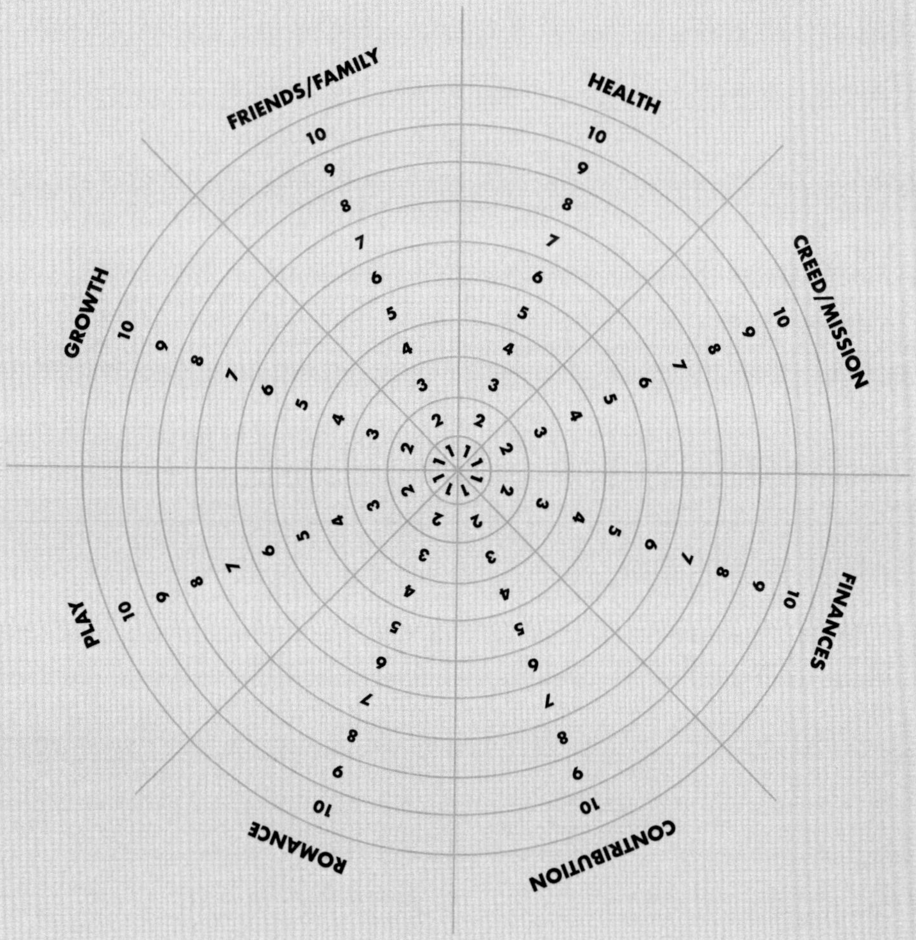
FRIENDS/FAMILY
HEALTH
CREED/MISSION
FINANCES
CONTRIBUTION
ROMANCE
PLAY
GROWTH

EXERCISE 2

YOUR BEST LIFE SCORECARD

The scorecard is another powerful tool designed to give you deeper insight. Each question has been thoughtfully crafted from my experiences coaching high-achieving men over 40, to target the areas that matter most for your growth.

By completing the scorecard, you'll receive personalised results and a tailored guide to support your journey towards greater freedom, clarity and purpose. You can access it here: www.cassandraandrews.com/scorecard

EXERCISE 3

THE JOHARI WINDOW

The Johari Window is a tool created by psychologists Joseph Luft and Harrington Ingham, that offers a framework for understanding self-awareness and interpersonal relationships.

It consists of four quadrants that represent different aspects of oneself, based on what is known or unknown to oneself and others:

- **Open Self:** This quadrant represents what you know about yourself and what others also know about you. It's your public persona, your traits, skills and behaviours that are transparent and recognised by both you and others.

- **Blind Self:** This quadrant includes things others know about you, but you are unaware of. These are your blind spots – traits or behaviours you may not realise you exhibit but are noticeable to others.
- **Hidden Self:** This quadrant consists of what you know about yourself but keep hidden from others. It's the part of you that you choose not to share, whether due to fear, insecurity or a desire for privacy.
- **Unknown Self:** This quadrant represents what is unknown to both you and others. It includes your untapped potential, hidden talents or unconscious behaviours and beliefs that neither you nor others are aware of yet.

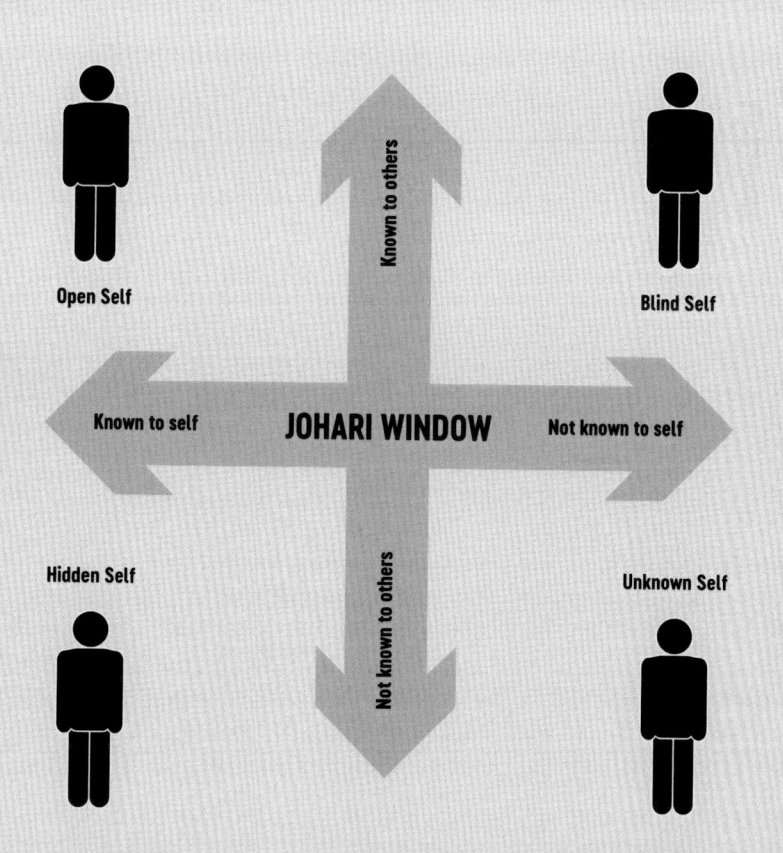

Open Self — Known to others / Known to self

Blind Self — Known to others / Not known to self

JOHARI WINDOW

Hidden Self — Known to self / Not known to others

Unknown Self — Not known to self / Not known to others

Let's see how Andrew used the Johari Window as part of his journey to becoming aware.

Open Self: Andrew began by reflecting on aspects of his life that were well-known to both him and others. He realised he'd had a fulfilling career and business, a loving family and good health. These are elements that he and those close to him recognise as contributing to his overall wellbeing. However, he also acknowledged that there may be areas where he could improve, such as prioritising self-care or pursuing personal passions outside of work.

Blind Self: Andrew sought feedback from his family, friends and trusted peers to uncover blind spots in his life. He asked questions like:

- What are some first impressions people might have about me that I may not realise?
- What qualities or traits do you think I have that I might not fully recognise in myself?
- What do you think is one area where I could grow or improve that I might not have considered?

Through those conversations, he learned that whilst he appeared to have it all together on the surface, there were underlying feelings of dissatisfaction and unfulfilled dreams. Others observed that he often prioritised work over personal fulfilment and regularly neglected his own needs for the sake of others. This feedback prompted Andrew to reassess his priorities and consider whether he was truly living in alignment with his values and aspirations and if indeed he was avoiding something.

Hidden Self: Andrew delved into aspects of himself that he was keeping hidden from others, as well as from himself. Upon introspection, he realised that he was suppressing his desire for adventure and exploration in favour of routine and security. He knew there were dreams he'd put aside over the years out of fear or complacency. Recognising these hidden desires prompted Andrew to re-evaluate his life vision and take steps to incorporate more joy and spontaneity into his life.

Unknown Self: Finally, Andrew reflected on the aspects of his life that may be unknown to both him and others. He considered the possibility that there were undiscovered passions or opportunities for growth waiting to be explored. This led him to embark on a journey of self-discovery through therapeutic coaching, trusting the process and embracing the journey with a sense of curiosity and openness.

By using the Johari Window as a framework for self-reflection, Andrew gained valuable insights into whether he was truly living his best life. Through reflection, feedback, and a willingness to explore the unknown, he took steps to align his actions with his values and aspirations, ultimately leading to a more fulfilling and authentic way of living.

Now it's your turn. The Johari Window is an invitation to delve into the layers of yourself that shape how you live, love and lead. As you explore each quadrant, allow yourself to uncover insights that may affirm, challenge or even surprise you.

Embrace it as an opportunity to step closer to your true self, one that's aligned, authentic and ready to live more fully.

I ASSUME YOU'VE HAD A GO AT SOME OF THE EXERCISES?

If not, pause here and consider what's stopping you. Is it that you want to race to the end of the chapter because you're a high achiever (and who needs to do these exercises anyway?). Maybe you think you haven't got time. Let's get real. You've picked up this book because you know that something isn't as you want it in your life. So cut the BS and be honest with yourself, because we always make time for what is important to us.

When I asked Andrew to do these exercises, he was initially cautious about what he might unpack. I explained to him that what he resists will always persist inside him, and wouldn't he rather be in control of how he lives his life, rather than under the control of the outdated programming of his five-year-old self? I also reassured him that his unconscious mind would never give him more than he could handle and even if it created some discomfort, he would always have the internal resources to manage it.

So, I encourage you to go back, pick an exercise that feels right for you, play with it and then come back here.

Okay. Well done. On behalf of your future self, I acknowledge you for your commitment to creating a life of freedom. There's one more exercise I'd like you to do. Ready to go deeper?

EXERCISE 4

SHIT LIST

This exercise is about getting real with yourself. It's about releasing everything that is getting in the way of you having the life you want – your emotions, beliefs, thoughts, internal conflicts, patterns and anything else you want to download.

Start by writing down everything that keeps you awake at night, the things that have never left your lips, your deepest secrets, the things that bring you pain, hurt, guilt or shame. Nobody is ever going to see this list (and you can always burn it if you want!) so get it all out because I promise you things look different on paper than they do in your head. It's really important that you write down everything that comes to mind, no matter how irrelevant it seems. List them all without editing and without any judgement of yourself.

If you'd like a structured guide for this exercise, it's available for download on my website: cassandraandrews.com/unlearning.

Here's just a few of the things that Andrew wrote on his shit list:

Andrew's Shit List

It's my responsibility to make everyone happy.

I thought that selling the business would feel like freedom, but I just feel lost.

I feel more like a roommate than a husband these days.

My fitness is nowhere near what it used to be, but I can't seem to prioritise it.

I'm just going through the motions.

All this success – does any of it even matter?

I don't know how to say what I feel.

Now that you have your shit list, take a moment to notice how your body feels. Does it feel lighter? Or perhaps it seems like the pressure has shifted slightly or maybe the pain in your shoulder feels slightly less intense.

This is an important part of the process because your thoughts, worries and concerns are stored in your body and it's important to recognise what might be causing or contributing to any physical pain you might have (more on this in Chapter Six).

Now shift your attention to what you have written. Are there any key emotions you're holding on to . . . guilt perhaps, or maybe anger or sadness? Recognising this is important because it starts to show you what might be driving your thoughts and behaviours.

Are there any key thoughts that could be a limiting belief? A limiting belief is a deeply held thought or assumption that restricts your potential, often based on past experiences or societal expectations. These beliefs create your world and who you believe you are and what you believe is possible for you (see Chapter Four).

For example, Andrew believed he had to make everyone happy, which he discovered stemmed from an idea that his worth and success are tied to constantly pleasing others. This belief developed from years of prioritising others' needs over his own. He believed if he wasn't making others happy, he was failing in his roles as a father, partner, employee or friend. It meant he felt taken for granted and was unable to set healthy boundaries for himself and pursue the things in life that were important to him.

Finished? Well done. Now, go and move your body. It doesn't matter what it is, go for a run, swim, walk, play a game of squash, anything that will create some movement to change your state and get the blood pumping!

YOUR UNLEARNING

If you truly want to live your best life, it begins with self-awareness. Here are some ideas to consider:

1. **Unlearn the belief** that your worth is tied to the roles you play for others.
2. **Unlearn the idea** that self-care is selfish and embrace it as essential.
3. **Unlearn the habit** of harsh self-criticism; treat yourself with the same kindness you'd offer a friend.
4. **Unlearn the need** to push through discomfort without pause; allow yourself patience and compassion as you navigate self-awareness.
5. **Unlearn the need** to numb or avoid emotions; instead, allow yourself to feel and grow.

CHAPTER THREE

YOU ARE NOT YOUR DAD

Imagine Andrew again. He's in his early fifties, sitting alone in the quiet of his living room. His children have moved out, his wife's gone to bed early and he's surrounded by the markers of a successful life. He's done everything 'right', he's achieved all he set out to do. Yet, as he sits there, he can't shake the nagging feeling that something feels off. It's not about money or status; he's got those. This feeling goes deeper, like he's been climbing someone else's mountain.

He thinks back to his own father, a man with a clear, unwavering set of values. Andrew realises he's spent years working to live up to those values without ever really questioning if they were his. And here he is, wondering if he's built a life that truly reflects who he is or one that honours the expectations of others.

Sound familiar? If so, you're not alone. When you reach your forties and beyond, life has a way of making you pause, nudging you to look inwards. You've been hustling for years, keeping everything together, achieving all you set out to accomplish. And yet, like many of my clients at this stage, you're finding yourself at the top of a mountain wondering if it's the right one. Success by society's standards isn't necessarily satisfying the craving for something more personal, something that feels real and purposeful.

That's where your values come in.

In this chapter, we're going to unpack what your values really are, how they've shaped you over the years and why they matter now more than ever. I'll ask you to reflect on some big questions and it may feel a bit uncomfortable. Stay with me though, I promise it'll be worth it. Because once you understand your values and start living in alignment with them, life stops feeling like something that happens *to* you. You're no longer just climbing; you're choosing the mountain. You become the one in the driver's seat, steering your life in a direction that feels authentic and full of purpose.

WHAT ARE VALUES?

Let's keep it simple – values are the things that matter most to you in life. They're deeply personal and are the core principles that shape how you live, what you prioritise and how you make decisions. Whether you realise it or not, they guide you every day, from the small choices you make to those big life-changing decisions.

Think of values as your personal GPS. They help you figure out where you're going and, more importantly, why you're heading in that direction. If you've ever felt a sense of purpose or clarity about something in your life, it's likely because you were acting in congruence with your values. On the flip side, if you've ever felt stuck or uneasy, that's probably because something was out of alignment with what truly matters to you.

What's interesting is that values aren't a one-size-fits-all. They're unique to you, shaped by your life experiences and what you've learned over time. Some men value family above all else, whilst others might prioritise financial success, health or personal growth. None of these are better or worse than others, they're just different ways of navigating life.

When you were younger, your values may have revolved around building a career, making a name for yourself, or gaining independence. This of course is totally natural. However, as you move through life, especially when you move in to your forties and beyond, things can start to shift. What once seemed so important, like chasing the next promotion or working extra hours, might not feel as fulfilling any more.

This is when you start to take stock. You might find that now you're more focused on things like meaningful connections, personal wellbeing or making a difference. You realise that time is precious, and you want to make sure you're spending it in ways that truly matter to you.

"If you've ever felt stuck or uneasy, that's probably because something was out of alignment with what truly matters to you"

That's the beauty of values; they evolve with you. As you grow, so do your priorities and this evolution is what helps you make sense of where you've been and where you want to go. Knowing your values gives you a sense of direction. They help you stay grounded, especially when life feels chaotic or when you're faced with tough decisions.

When you understand your values, decisions become easier. You know what's important and what's not, so you can let go of the things that don't serve you and focus on what brings you fulfilment. It's like cutting through the noise of daily life and getting straight to what matters most.

HOW ARE VALUES FORMED?

Values don't just appear out of nowhere. They're shaped over time, through a blend of experiences, relationships and reflections. To understand how values are formed, it's helpful to look at them as evolving in different stages:

The foundation or imprint period: Between the ages of approximately 0–7, your values started taking shape based on what you saw around you. The family you grew up in, the environment you were exposed to and the experiences you had during these formative years all created the foundation of your values.

During this time, you're like a sponge, absorbing everything around you. You observed how the adults in your life behaved, how they treated others, and what they prioritised. Perhaps kindness and empathy were valued in your home, or maybe you were taught to work hard and value success, or possibly community and connection were more central.

For Andrew, growing up in a home where his father's mantra was 'hard work always pays off', he learned early on that effort and achievement were the keys to being valued. Whether it was mowing the lawn perfectly or getting good grades, Andrew associated his worth with how much he accomplished. Similarly, he remembers his mother always putting others first, teaching him the value of selflessness but also leaving him with a belief that his own needs should come last.

You may not have been aware, but the lessons you were learning about right and wrong, fairness, kindness and hard work all began to take root. Just like Andrew, you likely absorbed these values without realising how deeply they would shape your choices later in life.

Testing the waters or modelling period: Between the ages of 7–14, as you moved into adolescence, you may have started to question the values you absorbed in childhood. This is a period of exploration, rebellion and experimentation. Teenagers often challenge their parents' values and try on new perspectives, like trying on clothes to see what fits. They're figuring out where they stand and what they want to take forward into adulthood.

For Andrew, this was the time he started pushing back against his father's strict emphasis on hard work. He remembers skipping his chores to play football with his friends and feeling torn between wanting to meet his father's expectations and carving out his own identity. He also recalls the influence of his peers, particularly a close group of boys who valued loyalty and sticking together no matter what.

During this time, your peers will have been incredibly influential as you began to develop values around independence, identity and belonging. Like Andrew, you might have started thinking more deeply about who you are and what you believe, outside of your family unit, as you began shaping the values that would guide you into adulthood.

The solidifying or socialisation period: Between the ages of 14–21, you likely began to establish a more stable sense of self. You tested different values during your teenage years and started to commit to some of them. This is the stage when you probably chose your career path, formed serious relationships, and made life decisions based on the values you began to prioritise.

For Andrew, this was the time he threw himself into working hard, taking on part-time jobs and long hours to prove he could stand on his own two feet. The value of hard work, ingrained since childhood, became his guiding principle. He believed that effort and perseverance were the keys to success and was determined to make his mark. Yet, there were moments when he questioned this approach; watching friends take a more laid-back path and still seem happy, he wondered if his relentless work ethic was worth the sacrifice.

However, these values were still somewhat fluid. They were influenced by the successes and failures Andrew experienced in early adulthood. For instance, getting recognised for his work reinforced his belief in hard work, but missing out on time with friends and relationships made him question whether he was prioritising the right things.

At this stage, you begin to see how your values shape your choices and impact your life. Like Andrew, the decisions you make during this time often set the foundation for what you'll prioritise as you move forward.

By the time you've reached midlife, you may find yourself reassessing your values. You may have started asking yourself, *What am I really here for? Is this truly the life I want to be living?* Values that once seemed paramount, like ambition, status or material success, may have begun to feel less important. You may find yourself valuing deeper connections, health, inner peace or leaving a legacy that extends beyond yourself.

'MEANS' AND 'ENDS' VALUES

By now you've probably done a lot of the 'right' things – built a career, maybe started a family, stayed committed to your goals. You're ticking the boxes. But sometimes, something still feels off. Despite all your efforts, the fulfilment you expected isn't always there.

This is where 'means' and 'ends' values come in. Understanding the difference can help you figure out why all your efforts might not be hitting the mark.

MEANS VALUES: THE 'HOW'

Means values are about 'how' you live your life. They're the tools and strategies you rely on to achieve your goals, like hard work, discipline or integrity. They guide your day-to-day actions.

For example, if you value hard work, you've likely put in the long hours and made sacrifices. But why are you working so hard? That's where ends values come in.

ENDS VALUES: THE 'WHY'

Ends values are the bigger picture, the reason behind all that hard work. These are the things that truly give life meaning, like happiness, connection or personal freedom – the ultimate outcome or feeling you want to achieve.

If you're working hard just for the sake of it, you're stuck on the means value. But if you're working hard to create financial security for your family or the freedom to retire early and travel, you've connected your means value (hard work) to your ends value (freedom, security or family).

WHY DOES THIS MATTER FOR YOU NOW?

The challenge for so many high-achieving men is that they've been living by their means values – working hard, staying disciplined, doing all the things society says they should – but haven't spent enough time thinking about their ends values. The result? You might find yourself feeling like you're constantly grinding, but you're not sure what all the effort is for any more.

Take Andrew, for example. For years, he prided himself on his relentless work ethic, often pulling late nights and sacrificing holidays to meet deadlines and build his business. Hard work was his mantra, it made him feel accomplished and in control. When Andrew started to question why he'd been working so hard, he realised that while he was chasing success, what he really wanted was freedom; the ability to step off the treadmill and spend time with his family or simply take a day off without guilt. This shift helped him see that his hard work (a means value) wasn't aligned with his deeper desire for freedom (an ends value).

It's like taking a road trip. If you're so focused on driving fast and staying on course and don't ask where you're headed, you might end up somewhere you don't want to be. The drive (your means values) is important, but the destination (your ends values) is what really matters.

So, take some time to reflect. What are your means values – those behaviours that drive you day-to-day? And what are your ends values – the big, meaningful outcomes that give your life purpose?

To start, think about one or two things you've been focusing on recently. Then ask yourself:

- Why is this important to me?
- What am I hoping to achieve or feel as a result of this?

Often, the first answer will point to a means value (like discipline or hard work), but as you go deeper, you'll uncover your ends value whether it's security, freedom, connection or something else. This is the beginning of aligning your effort with your purpose.

Later in this chapter, we'll explore a structured exercise to help you dig deeper and uncover your core values. For now, this reflection is a small step towards clarity.

'TOWARDS' AND 'AWAY FROM' VALUES

Now that we've covered 'means' and 'ends' values – how you get to where you want to go and why you're doing it – let's take this a step further. Understanding what drives you isn't just about knowing your goals or how you'll achieve them. It's also about understanding the deeper forces behind your choices. Are you being pulled towards something you truly want, or are you just trying to avoid something you fear? That's where 'towards' and 'away from' values come in.

At their core, 'towards' and 'away from' values both revolve around two primal human motivators: seeking pleasure and avoiding pain. Understanding this concept can really help you see if your values are working for or against you and why you might just keep getting stuck.

'TOWARDS' VALUES: WHAT PULLS YOU FORWARD

'Towards' values are the things that get you out of bed in the morning. These are the values that pull you towards the life you want (pleasure). They're the positive outcomes you desire, whether that's health, connection, freedom or growth. When you live by your towards values, you're motivated by what excites and fulfils you, the things that make you feel like you're building something meaningful.

For example, maybe health is a towards value for you. You're driven to stay fit and active, not just to avoid illness, but because you want to feel strong, energised and alive. You enjoy the process of staying healthy and it's pulling you towards a life where you can be at your best for yourself and the people around you.

Or take connection as another example. You value deep, meaningful relationships, and you're motivated to spend time with the people you care about, have real conversations and build a sense of community. That's a towards value – it's something you want more of in your life, and it pulls you forward towards the experiences and relationships that matter most to you.

'AWAY FROM' VALUES: WHAT YOU'RE TRYING TO AVOID

On the other side are 'away from' values. These are the things you're trying to avoid, perhaps failure, rejection or stress (pain). Away from values are about steering clear of what you don't want. They often come from a place of fear, loss or discomfort and whilst they can be powerful motivators, they can also leave you feeling like you're constantly running away from something, rather than moving towards something fulfilling.

For instance, maybe you're motivated by a desire to avoid failure. You work hard, you push yourself and you stay on top of everything, but it's because you're afraid of falling short, not because you're chasing a specific goal. That's an away from value. It keeps you moving, but it's driven by fear of what might happen if you don't work hard enough, rather than a clear idea of what you truly want to achieve.

Or maybe you've spent years avoiding conflict in your relationships. You keep the peace, even when it means staying quiet or letting things slide, because conflict makes you uncomfortable. That's an away from value too. You're not focusing on building deeper connections or understanding, you're just trying to avoid the tension and discomfort that comes with tough conversations.

WHY THIS MATTERS FOR YOU

At this stage in life, when you've already achieved so much, it's time to get honest with yourself about what's been driving you. Have you been living your life pulled forward by what you want, or have you been reacting to what you're trying to avoid? This distinction matters because it can explain why, even after years of hard work, something still feels off.

If you've been motivated by 'away from' values like avoiding failure or conflict, you might have achieved a lot, but I'm guessing you don't feel truly fulfilled. Yes, you've steered clear of the things you didn't want, but have you really been moving towards the things that bring you joy, meaning and freedom?

OVER TO YOU . . .

GETTING CLARITY ON WHAT TRULY DRIVES YOU

We've explored why values matter and how they shape the direction of your life, so let's now apply this to your own values because taking time to explore what's pulling you forward and what you're trying to avoid is one of the greatest gifts you can give yourself.

To help with this, I want to share with you a powerful technique I use with my clients.

The process is simple, but it does require you to be honest with yourself. By following the steps below you'll be able to dig beneath the surface and identify the core values driving your actions, decisions and motivation. Once you get clarity, you'll be able to make choices that align with who you are and what you truly want right now in your life.

STEP ONE.

Identify a key area of your life: Start by choosing an important area of your life that you want to explore. I often recommend starting with your overall life values and then moving to more specific areas such as business, health, money, relationships, etc.

STEP TWO.

Ask yourself what's important: Once you've chosen your area of focus, for example 'life', take out your journal and ask yourself this simple but powerful question:

'What's important to me about [this area] right now?'

Start by writing down as many values as possible; for example, if you were looking at your life values, you might write: choice, peace, health, fun . . . The first few words that come to mind are often the most obvious but keep going, even if it feels like you're running out of ideas. No judgement, no pressure, just keep listing until you have around 30 to 60 values. If you're struggling, think about anything you consistently prioritise in this area. Chances are, that's a reflection of your values.

STEP THREE.

Prioritise your values: Once you've uncovered your core values for your chosen area, it's time to prioritise them.

- Ask yourself which of these values is most important. Circle about 8–10 values that resonate the strongest.
- Next, rank the chosen 8–10 values in order of importance.
- Now, to ensure you are tapping into your true wants and not clouded by what you think you *should* want, it's important that you compare each of these values against the next in the list by asking yourself:

'If I could only have one of these, which would it be?'

For example, take your top two values and ask yourself, 'If I could only have one of these things which would it be?' Keep doing this with all your selected values until you have them arranged in a clear order of priority.

This process helps you see which values truly take precedence in your life. You might find some surprises, or you may confirm what you've always known deep down.

When Andrew first started working with me, we looked at his values, which was one of the first times he'd ever got curious about what he really wanted. We established that his values in order were:

1. **Success**
2. **Freedom**
3. **Family**
4. **Health**
5. **Legacy**
6. **Impact**
7. **Security**
8. **Balance**

I then asked Andrew, 'If you could only have one, success or freedom, which would you choose?' This forced him to get really honest about what mattered to him now.

Andrew hesitated. For most of his life, success had been his top priority. But now, when he compared it to freedom, something inside him shifted. 'I think I'd choose freedom,' he said slowly. 'I've been working so hard for so long, but what I really want now is to get off the hamster wheel and have control over my time, to do what I want, when I want.' That realisation surprised him, as he'd never questioned his drive for success before. But as he thought about it, he could feel the weight of years of constant striving. Freedom was starting to mean more.

Then, I compared freedom to family: 'If you could only have one, freedom or family, which would it be?' This one was easier for Andrew, as family took the top spot without hesitation. He reflected on how much time he'd missed with his children as they grew up, how many family moments had passed him by while he was tied up in meetings or working late at the office. 'I can't get that time back,' he said, 'but I don't want to miss any more.'

We continued through the list, comparing values like health and legacy. Andrew realised that his health had been neglected for too long. He had always pushed it aside, thinking he could focus on it later. But now, with family and freedom climbing up his priority list, he saw that if he didn't take care of his health, he wouldn't be able to enjoy it either.

By the time we finished, Andrew's list of values looked very different than when he started.

1. Success	1. **Family**
2. Freedom	2. **Health**
3. Family	3. **Freedom**
4. Health	4. **Legacy**
5. Legacy	5. **Success**
6. Impact	6. **Balance**
7. Security	7. **Impact**
8. Balance	8. **Security**

Andrew left that session with a new sense of clarity. He wasn't abandoning his career or his success, rather he was realigning his focus. Now the choices he would make would be based on what truly mattered to him; he wouldn't be just chasing success for success's sake, but rather creating a life where his values of family, health and freedom took the lead.

STEP FOUR.

Check for 'towards' and 'away from' values: Now you've prioritised your values, it's important to check if they're towards or away from values. Are you being driven by the desire for something (pleasure), or are you trying to avoid something (pain)? To help you figure this out, ask yourself:

'What's important to me about that?' or 'What's the purpose of that?'

'What percentage am I moving towards this value and what percentage am I moving away?'

'Does this value feel light and inspiring, or heavy and stressful?'

For example, if security is a value in your business, are you moving towards a feeling of peace and freedom that security brings, or are you avoiding the fear of losing control or not providing for your family? Identifying this will help you understand whether your motivations are towards or away from values.

When you've done this, you'll have a completed list of values.

STEP FIVE.

What's missing: Looking at your values, ask yourself if anything is missing. For example, if you long to feel free of responsibility, but your top life values are business, success and money, you may need to add in a value that helps move you towards freedom.

This part of the exercise involves working with the unconscious mind, so I recommend you contact an NLP Master Practitioner who can help you add or remove values to ensure they are aligned and congruent with who you want to be on a deeper level.

Our current values often reflect what we've prioritised in the past, but they don't always match what we need or desire moving forward. This step goes deeper than just listing values on the surface; it works with the unconscious mind, where your values are stored and where the real magic happens.

Take the example above. You might consciously want freedom yet find yourself continually driven by deeply rooted values of financial security or success. These unconscious patterns can create a gap between what you think you want and what your unconscious mind is actually prioritising. Closing that gap is where transformation begins.

It's not unusual to approach this with some scepticism, but the experience is often profoundly eye-opening. Many of my clients have described it as a moment of deep clarity, a chance to understand themselves on a level they didn't even realise existed.

STEP SIX.

Repeat for other areas of your life: Now that you've gone through this process in one area of your life, you can repeat the same steps for other areas; for example, relationships, business, health etc. Each might reveal different values than you were expecting. However, together they'll give you a more complete picture of what truly drives you in different areas of your life.

This process of eliciting your values is about giving you the clarity to live in congruence with what's most important to you. By understanding what motivates you, both in terms of what you want more of and what you're avoiding, you'll be in a much stronger position to make decisions that feel right, purposeful and true to who you are.

YOUR UNLEARNING

Here are some takeaways to help you unlearn old patterns and make room for values that genuinely resonate with you:

1. **Unlearn inherited expectations**: Let go of values you've absorbed from family, especially those you haven't consciously chosen, and begin to understand what truly matters to *you*.
2. **Unlearn focusing only on the 'means' value:** Recognise where you've been driven by values like hard work or discipline (the how) without connecting them to a meaningful end or purpose (the why).
3. **Unlearn 'away from' motivations**: Shift from being driven by avoiding failure or discomfort and begin pursuing values that pull you towards joy, freedom and purpose.
4. **Unlearn outdated priorities**: Reassess values you once prioritised, like ambition or status, that may no longer resonate and realign with what feels authentic and meaningful now.
5. **Unlearn society's definitions of success**: Move beyond societal expectations and redefine success based on values that feel personal, grounded and in line with the life you genuinely want to create.

CHAPTER FOUR

I SHOULD BE ABLE TO PLAY GUITAR BY NOW

Andrew sat on the edge of his bed, eyeing the guitar propped against the wall. He'd bought it 10 years ago, convinced that learning to play was part of becoming a well-rounded man; the kind of man who could relax, let loose and enjoy life outside the boardroom. But here it was, untouched, gathering dust. 'I should be able to play guitar by now,' he muttered to himself.

That thought echoed a list of other quiet expectations he'd stacked on his shoulders:

'People expect me to have all the answers,' 'You can't rely on anyone but yourself,' 'Slowing down is a sign of failure' and 'I'm responsible for everyone else's happiness.'

Sound familiar? Perhaps you've had similar beliefs that may have fuelled your achievements and helped you build a life others admire. However, whilst these beliefs may have served you once, it's worth asking: are they still serving you now? Or have they turned into invisible chains, trapping you in cycles of overthinking, stress and self-doubt?

In your forties and fifties, the rules that once guided you may no longer apply. Yet these beliefs can feel set in stone, so embedded that you might not even recognise them as choices. But that's exactly what they are.

"Beliefs aren't fixed truths; they're simply thoughts repeated until they've become your reality. What's exciting is that you have the power to change them."

This chapter is about one thing: beliefs – the stories you've been telling yourself your entire life. The beliefs and rules you've created as the foundation upon which you've built your world. Every decision, every goal and every challenge has been filtered through their lens. We'll explore what beliefs are, how they've shaped your reality, and the difference between empowering beliefs (the ones that fuel your growth) and limiting beliefs (the ones that keep you stuck).

By the end of this chapter, you'll have the tools to identify and transform these limiting beliefs, reshaping the internal narrative that has held you back. You'll be able to start building a belief system that aligns with the life you want to live.

WHAT ARE BELIEFS AND HOW ARE THEY FORMED?

In the previous chapter we explored values – the deep principles that guide your life, the things that are important to you. Beliefs are the stories you tell yourself about how the world works. Both are central to who you are; however, they work in different ways to shape your life and the sense of who you believe you are.

The real challenge comes when beliefs don't align with your values; for example, if you value freedom but believe, 'I have to work non-stop to be successful.' When this happens, life can feel out of sync.

Imagine beliefs like an inner framework that's shaping your perception of the world. They act as a lens through which you interpret every experience, relationship and opportunity. At their core, beliefs are the assumptions and convictions you hold about yourself, others and life in general. They guide your thoughts, influence your emotions and, most importantly, dictate your actions. These mental 'rules' govern how you interact with the world, often without you even realising it. They're powerful, not because they are true, but because, you *believe* them to be true.

Beliefs are formed through a combination of life experiences, messages from others, societal norms and conditioning. From an early age, you began absorbing ideas from your parents, teachers and peers about what's expected, what's right, what's wrong and what's possible. These ideas solidify over time, turning into the rules you live by.

The truth is, not every belief we hold is fact-based or beneficial. Sometimes, beliefs are formed out of necessity or survival, often from a young age when we have fewer tools to navigate complex emotions. These beliefs when carried forward into adulthood, can become limiting, no longer reflecting who we are or what we want out of life.

Let's look at a practical example. Roger Bannister was the first man to run a mile in under four minutes. Before Bannister's famous run in 1954, the idea of running a mile in under four minutes was not only seen as impossible, it was believed to be dangerous. Coaches, athletes and even doctors had long warned that attempting such a feat could cause physical harm or even death. For years, athletes came close, but no one could break that seemingly unbreakable barrier. The belief that it simply couldn't be done was so deeply ingrained that it became a mental block for runners around the world.

Bannister, however, had a different belief. Despite the widespread conviction that the four-minute mile was a wall no human could scale, Bannister questioned that assumption. Instead of accepting the belief that it was impossible, he chose to see it as a challenge – something that could be overcome with the right mindset and preparation. He didn't just train his body; he trained his mind to reject the limitations others had accepted as truth.

On 6th May 1954, Roger Bannister ran a mile in 3 minutes and 59.4 seconds, breaking the four-minute barrier and proving that the limits we accept are often more mental than physical. What's even more fascinating is what happened after Bannister's achievement. Once he had proven it was possible, other runners followed suit. Within 46 days, another runner, John Landy, broke Bannister's record. By the end of that year, several others had also run a mile in under four minutes. Today, breaking the four-minute mile is a standard achievement for elite runners. What had once been considered impossible is now routinely accomplished.

In your own life, you may have accepted similar mental barriers; for example, 'success only comes through constant struggle'. But just as Bannister questioned the accepted limits of his time, you have the power to challenge the beliefs that have shaped your reality. What's limiting you may not be the external circumstances, rather the internal narrative that tells you those limits are fixed and unchangeable.

Bannister's story reminds us that beliefs are not facts. They are simply thoughts we've repeated to ourselves or adopted from others until they seem like truth. The moment you begin to question them, you open the door to new possibilities. Possibilities that may have been right in front of you all along but were hidden by the mental filters of your beliefs.

When Andrew was growing up, his parents constantly told him, 'You have to work hard for everything you want in life.' This wasn't just a casual remark; it was a deep-rooted message reinforced every day. He saw it in the way his parents worked long hours, rarely taking time for themselves, always focused on providing and pushing forward. His wider family echoed the same sentiment, and society added its own pressure, praising those who never seemed to stop, who wore their exhaustion like a badge of honour.

Over time, this idea sank in and became more than just advice, it became a core belief – 'Success requires relentless hard work.'. It wasn't something he consciously chose, it just became the lens through which he viewed the world. Andrew believed that slowing down, even for a moment, meant falling behind. Rest? That was for people who weren't serious about achieving real success. And so, he pushed himself harder and harder, often at the expense of his health and wellbeing, convinced that if he ever let up, it would all fall apart.

This belief shaped every decision he made, driving him to work late into the night, sacrifice family time and constantly chase the next goal, because in his mind, anything less was failure. It didn't matter how exhausted he felt or how much stress weighed on him, Andrew truly believed that constant pushing was the only way to achieve anything of real value.

TYPES OF BELIEF

Beliefs can be categorised based on their focus – whether they're about you, other people or the world at large. These different types of beliefs influence how you interact with yourself, others and life in general. Understanding these three types can help you identify where your beliefs are impacting your life the most and which ones may need a closer look.

BELIEFS ABOUT YOURSELF

What do you believe about 'you'? These are the beliefs that shape how you see yourself, your potential and your limitations. As a high achiever, maybe like Andrew you've always believed, *I have to keep pushing, or I'll lose everything I've worked for.* Sound familiar? That belief probably helped you build your career, but now it might be keeping you stuck in the fast lane, never allowing you to slow down and actually enjoy the success you've earned.

Here's another one that might hit home: I can't rely on anyone else – they'll just let me down. Maybe you've been burned before; someone you trusted let you down or a business deal went wrong. So now, the belief is: I have to do it all. Whilst that belief might have made you independent and driven, it's also probably left you feeling drained and disconnected, constantly managing everything on your own. It can make delegating or asking for help feel like a weakness, which means you end up carrying more than you need to, both at work and in your personal life.

BELIEFS ABOUT OTHERS

Now let's talk about what you believe about other people. Maybe you've been telling yourself, *No one can do it as well as I can* or *If I don't handle this, it won't get done right*. That belief might have fuelled your success, but it can also leave you feeling like you're carrying the weight of the world on your shoulders.

What about the belief, *People expect me to have all the answers*. This one's tricky. On one hand, it's probably true that people look up to you for guidance and leadership. But the belief that you always have to have it together can leave you feeling isolated and exhausted. It stops you from letting people in, from showing vulnerability, or from even admitting when you don't have all the answers.

BELIEFS ABOUT LIFE IN GENERAL

Finally, there's what you believe about life itself. Maybe you've lived by the belief that *Success only comes from constant hard work*. That belief pushed you to achieve, but now does it feel like it's become a prison? Like there's never an off switch, even when you want to slow down and enjoy life?

Here's another one to think about: *Life's a competition and if I don't stay ahead, I'll fall behind.* Maybe that belief has driven you to always be on your game, pushing for the next goal, the next promotion or the next big win. But over time, this constant need to stay ahead can leave you feeling like you're always on the edge, never able to relax or feel secure in your achievements.

This belief might have fuelled your ambition, but it can also make life feel like a never-ending race, with no room to breathe. It also keeps you on the hamster wheel, constantly comparing yourself to others, always worrying about whether you're doing enough, having enough or being enough.

EARLY BELIEFS AND HOW THEY SHAPE YOUR LIFE TODAY

Many of the beliefs that shape your decisions as an adult have roots in your early years. When you were young, you absorbed lessons about how the world works, how to fit in and what was expected of you. These early beliefs often developed out of necessity or survival, helping you navigate life when you had fewer tools and less control over your circumstances. While we'll talk more about how to work with your 'inner child' later on, here we'll focus on how those early beliefs might still be influencing you today.

Think back to when you were growing up. Every experience, whether positive or negative, left a mark on how you saw the world. Maybe you learned that working hard earned praise, or that staying quiet kept you safe. For instance, if you felt you needed to earn approval through achievements, that belief may still drive you now, tying your worth to how much you accomplish, or the status symbols you accumulate.

Perhaps emotions weren't openly discussed in your household. If you were told to 'toughen up' or 'stop being so sensitive', you may have developed a belief that real men don't talk about feelings. As an adult, this belief might make it difficult to open up, even with people closest to you. You may have built your life around being tough and self-reliant, following an early script that suggested vulnerability wasn't safe.

For many of my clients, these early beliefs also shaped how they viewed money and success, leading to patterns that limited how much they enjoyed what they'd achieved. Imagine you grew up in a home where money was tight, and financial worry was always present. Maybe you heard things like, 'We can't afford that'; over time, you may have adopted the belief that there's never enough money. This belief might push you to work tirelessly, always in pursuit of more security, even when you've reached a point of stability. You might find it hard to relax, worrying that everything could disappear at any moment, caught in a cycle of overwork and stress, unable to fully enjoy the life you've built.

The reality is these early beliefs made sense in the context of your childhood. They were tools that helped you navigate an unpredictable world. However, as an adult, these outdated beliefs may keep you stuck in cycles of overwork, isolation or self-criticism. Recognising that these beliefs stem from early experiences helps you see them for what they are – outdated rules that no longer have to dictate your life.

EMPOWERING VS. LIMITING BELIEFS

Now that we've looked at how your childhood shaped many of your core beliefs, it's time to explore the two types of beliefs that shape your life: empowering beliefs and limiting beliefs. These are the beliefs that determine whether you're moving forward or staying stuck.

Let's start with empowering beliefs. These are the beliefs that lift you up, energise you and support your growth. They're the thoughts that give you confidence and clarity, allowing you to take on new challenges without feeling overwhelmed. An empowering belief might be something like, *I deserve the success I've worked for*. These beliefs create space for opportunity and new experiences. They help you move forward with purpose and enthusiasm, knowing that you're capable of evolving and growing, no matter where you are in life.

On the flipside, there are limiting beliefs, the ones that keep you stuck. These are the thoughts that act as invisible barriers in your mind, preventing you from fully enjoying your success or taking on new opportunities. They often stem from fear, designed to protect you from disappointment or failure. For example, maybe you've told yourself, *I need to keep pushing, or I'll lose my edge*. That belief might have served you well when you were younger, hustling to build your career or business. But now? It could be locking you into a cycle of overwork and stress, even though you're ready to embrace more freedom and fulfilment.

These limiting beliefs can feel so ingrained, like facts, when really, they're just outdated stories. Just as Roger Bannister shattered the belief that no one could run a mile in under four minutes, you too can break through your own limiting beliefs and replace them with ones that align with the life you truly want to live.

OVER TO YOU . . .

IDENTIFYING YOUR LIMITING BELIEFS

Ready? Let's dive into the beliefs that might be holding you back. Remember, this is your journey – you can move at your own pace and if anything feels challenging, know that you're in control. You can always take a step back, reflect and pick it up again when you're ready. Beliefs often give us a sense of security and identity, so it's normal to feel some discomfort as you begin to question them. Don't worry if that happens, it's all part of the process of growth and healing.

When I work with clients, I work directly with their unconscious mind, helping them delete any limiting beliefs using a powerful technique called Timeline Therapy. I believe this to be a quick and powerful way to create the change you want in your life.

As we're not together in person for this part of the process, we're going 'old school' and we're going to use a couple of techniques to help you loosen up your unconscious mind, because the first step to changing any belief is becoming aware of it. **This is a big exercise, so create some space.** I promise you it will be worth it.

STEP ONE.

Identify a specific area of life: Start by choosing part of your life where you're feeling stuck or frustrated. It could be anything – your career / business, relationships, health, etc. If you've already done the Wheel of Life exercise from Chapter Two, this is a great time to pick the area you want to focus on.

STEP TWO.

Uncover your limiting beliefs: Once you've chosen the area, grab your journal and do a brain dump. List all the things you believe about this part of your life. Include both the empowering beliefs (the ones that energise you) and the limiting ones (the ones that hold you back or feel heavy). Let everything flow out, don't judge it, don't filter it. Just get it all on the page.

To help you loosen up your unconscious and uncover those hidden beliefs, ask yourself the following questions about the area:

- What do I believe about myself here?
- What do I believe about others here?
- What do I believe about life here?
- What doubts do I have about this?
- What could be holding me back?
- What am I avoiding in this area?
- What negative chatter is on repeat?

Your statements might start with: I am, I can't, I have to, I should, I'm not, I always, I'm never, If I . . . then I . . .

STEP THREE.

Challenge the belief: Go back through your list and pick two beliefs that feel the heaviest – the ones that make your chest tighten or your shoulders sink just reading them. These are the beliefs that have been quietly shaping your life, perhaps more than you've realised. Circle them.

Now, for each of these beliefs, let's dig deeper with these questions. Take your time; we're uncovering decades of programming.

- **Is this belief actually true?** Or is it kind of ridiculous when I say it out loud?
- **What evidence do I have that proves this belief wrong?** Think back to moments in your life when this belief wasn't true. Journal even the smallest examples. The cracks in the foundation of your belief are proof that it's not as solid as it seems.
- **Where did this belief come from? Whose voice is it?** A parent, teacher, friend? Ask yourself: *Do they deserve to have this much influence on my life today?* This is your chance to separate their story from yours.
- **How has this belief negatively impacted my life so far?** Write down three specific moments when this belief made you hesitate, hold back or settle for less. What opportunities did you say no to, what decisions did you avoid? (Lean into this discomfort for a moment. It's not about dwelling on pain but feeling enough of it to create leverage for change. Be courageous, my friend. Growth often starts in the places we'd rather not look.)
- **What will it cost me emotionally, physically and financially if I keep holding onto this belief?** Imagine the ripple effects if this belief stays in control.
  - **Emotionally:** What will you miss out on? Peace, joy, connection?
  - **Physically:** How does carrying this belief impact your energy, stress levels, or health?

- **Financially:** How might this belief limit your earning potential or career growth?

Lean in again. This isn't about scaring yourself; it's about waking yourself up. Imagine this cost intensely. Write it down in detail. Let this clarity become your leverage to move forward.

READY TO GO DEEPER?

STEP FOUR.

Imagine the future: I can't stress enough the importance of this part of the exercise; it's where real emotional leverage happens. If you're anything like me, you might need a little help to really feel the weight of what this future could look like. Personally, I like to crank up some really emotive music, something that pulls on my heartstrings or gives me goosebumps. It helps me step into the moment fully, to see and feel exactly what's at stake if I don't choose differently. (Think movie montage, but with higher stakes!)

Now, take a deep breath and close your eyes. Imagine yourself 5, 10, even 20 years from now. This belief, the one that's been holding you back, is still dictating your choices, running your life and keeping you trapped in the same tired patterns. Step into that future and let the weight of it hit you.

What do you see? Look around. Does it feel weirdly familiar? The same routines, the same struggles, the same excuses. Maybe you're in the same house, at the same desk, in the same life, but everything feels smaller, like the walls have closed in. The opportunities you dreamed about are nowhere to be seen. Your world feels stagnant, empty, lifeless. Even if on the surface you've achieved more, does it feel hollow? Are you surrounded by things, but completely alone? Is there a part of you that can't even bear to meet your own gaze in the mirror because deep down, you know you wasted the opportunity to choose differently?

What do you hear? Is the silence deafening? Maybe you hear the echo of your own thoughts, that same self-defeating voice laughing at you: 'You're stuck. You'll never change. This is all there is for you.' Do you hear the voices of others? A wife who's now distant, tired of trying to connect with someone who wouldn't let them in. Children who don't call any more because they've given up on the relationship you never prioritised. Colleagues or friends who got sick of you cancelling on them.

What do you feel? Take another deep breath and immerse yourself in the emotions. Perhaps a heaviness in your chest, a gnawing ache in your stomach, or tension in your shoulders that never seems to leave. Is it regret? Frustration? Shame? The deep, paralysing realisation that you've been watching your own life pass you by. Feel the resentment, not just towards others, but towards yourself. You knew this belief was holding you back and you let it stay. Feel the hopelessness of knowing time has moved on without you. Imagine the bitterness of watching someone else, someone with less talent, less drive, live the life you secretly wanted, because they didn't let fear win.

And then the final blow. Who's no longer in your life because of this belief? Perhaps a wife who couldn't keep waiting for you to show up. Children who feel like they barely know you. Friends who stopped reaching out because they only ever got the surface-level you.

The risks you never took, the dreams you buried, the joy you convinced yourself wasn't possible. Feel the emptiness of those lost chances; the love you didn't fight for, the book you didn't write or the adventure you didn't go on because you thought it wasn't the right time. Picture yourself sitting alone, surrounded by the life you settled for and let the regret wash over you like a suffocating weight.

Is this a future you're willing to live with? Let the reality of this future sink in. Know that this is what happens if you don't change now. You're not here to punish yourself, you're here to wake yourself up. If this future feels unbearable, good. Use that pain. Let it give you the leverage you need to break free from the belief that's been holding you back.

Because right now, you have a choice: rewrite the story or let it control you.

Shit...... I told you this was a big exercise!

Take a moment to breathe and let it sink in.......

STEP FIVE.

Dissociate from the belief: Before we reframe the belief, let's loosen its grip on you. The goal here is to separate yourself from this belief so it no longer feels like an unchangeable truth. Instead, it becomes what it truly is: just a thought you've carried for too long.

Start by closing your eyes and creating a picture in your mind's eye to represent this old belief. What does it look like – is it in colour, big or small, like a movie or a still, is there sound, maybe a voice? Are there any feelings?

Now, play with it. Make the image black and white and blurry, then shrink it down to the size of a postage stamp. If there's sound, turn it down, so you can't hear it. If there's a voice, make it the silliest voice you can imagine (think helium!).

As you do this, notice how the belief feels less intense. Finally, take hold of this image and throw it away, far, far into the distance. Open your eyes and take a deep breath and then shake out your body. Congratulations my friend, you've created space for a new belief, one that will move you towards the life you want.

STEP SIX.

Reframe the belief: You've seen where this belief will take you if you let it run your life. Now, it's time to choose differently and take control of your future.

Start by writing down your old limiting belief, then take a pen and cross it out. Hard. Draw a bold, thick line through it, as if you're erasing any remaining power it has over you.

Now ask yourself:

- What would I prefer to believe instead?
- What belief could help me move forward, one step at a time?
- What truth about myself have I ignored because I've been too focused on this limitation?

This isn't about wishful thinking; it's about creating a perspective grounded in possibility and growth. Choose a belief that shifts your focus from fear to possibility. Write your new belief below the old one.

For example:

Limiting belief: 'I'm responsible for everyone else's happiness.' Reframed belief: 'I can support and care for my loved ones; however, their happiness is ultimately their own responsibility.'

Take the new belief and underline it. Circle it. Make it stand out. Let it become a statement of intention, a declaration of the life you're choosing to create.

STEP SEVEN.

Anchor the new belief: Now that you've reframed your limiting belief into something empowering, it's time to lock it in. Anchoring is a simple yet powerful NLP technique that helps embed your new belief into your mind by associating it with a strong positive emotion. Think of it like creating a shortcut in your brain. When you activate the anchor, you'll instantly reconnect with the confidence and power of your new belief.

By anchoring your new belief, you'll strengthen it and help it stick, so it becomes part of your everyday thinking and behaving.

- **Get into a positive emotional state** – to make the new belief stick, you need to associate it with a moment when you felt your best. Stand up, if possible, take a deep breath and think about a time in your life when you felt confident, in control or deeply fulfilled. Perhaps it's a moment of success, a proud achievement or a time you felt unstoppable.
- **Close your eyes and really immerse yourself in that moment.** See what you saw, hear what you heard and feel what you felt. Let yourself fully experience that positive emotion again. The more vivid the memory, the stronger the emotional anchor.
- **Create a physical trigger** – while you're in this positive state, prepare to create a simple physical gesture to act as your anchor. I suggest something subtle, like pressing a finger on one of your knuckles. This gesture will become your cue to reconnect with the positive emotions and the power of your new belief whenever you need it.
- **Set the new belief** – whilst holding onto this positive emotional state, repeat your new empowering belief to yourself. Say it out loud, with confidence and conviction and press your finger on your knuckle or whatever anchor you have decided to use. (You might want to find a quiet, private space to do this!)
- **Repeat** – do this process 5–10 times. The more you practise, the stronger the anchor becomes. Any time you feel yourself slipping into an old limiting belief, use your physical trigger (e.g. press your knuckle and you will feel a strong emotional connection to your new empowering belief).

Anchoring helps you bridge the gap between intention and action, making your new belief feel natural and accessible in your daily life. It's not just a thought any more, it's who you are becoming.

STEP EIGHT.

Rewrite the future: Now imagine stepping into your future 5, 10 or even 20 years from now. But this time, you're guided by your new empowering belief. How do you show up differently in your work, relationships or life? What do you see? What do you hear? What do you feel?

STEP NINE.

Final reflection: Ask yourself, 'What's one action I can take today to move closer to the future I've just imagined?' Write it down and commit to doing it within the next 24 hours.

WELL DONE. HOW ARE YOU DOING?

GO AND MOVE YOUR BODY.

BY THE WAY YOUR FUTURE SELF IS PROUD OF YOU.

YOUR UNLEARNING

Reflecting on this chapter, consider these key beliefs to unlearn, helping you to break free from old patterns and step into a space that truly supports a life of freedom.

1. **Unlearn the idea that your beliefs are unchangeable truths.** Beliefs are simply repeated thoughts that shape your reality, not facts.
2. **Unlearn the belief that your views on yourself, others and life are fixed.** Recognising and challenging these types of beliefs opens the door to a more flexible, fulfilling perspective on life.
3. **Unlearn limiting beliefs that conflict with your values.** When beliefs don't align with what you truly value, they create tension and dissatisfaction.
4. **Unlearn beliefs formed out of survival or past necessity.** Some beliefs were created to protect or guide you in earlier stages of life but may no longer serve your current vision.
5. **Unlearn the assumption that all success requires relentless struggle.** While hard work is valuable, allowing yourself moments of rest and joy doesn't undermine your achievements, it enhances your resilience and fulfilment.

CHAPTER FIVE

SHOULD I SELL THE PORSCHE?

Andrew settled into the driver's seat of his Porsche, the engine's quiet hum filling the silence as he stared through the windscreen. He should have felt the thrill, that familiar surge of pride and excitement. This car had been his statement to the world, proof that he'd made it. But as he gripped the wheel, he couldn't shake an unexpected feeling, a hollowness he hadn't noticed before. *Is this really what I want?* he found himself thinking.

The Porsche had once been everything to him, a badge of honour, the ultimate reward for years of relentless work. But today, it felt more like a mask, something that suited a past version of himself, not the man he was becoming. He wondered if he'd outgrown it, and for the first time, he entertained the idea of letting it go; not as a loss, but as a step towards something that actually felt real.

In this chapter, we're diving into that exact feeling: the sense of disconnect when the markers of success – status, wealth, recognition – no longer feel satisfying. Like Andrew, you might be reaching a moment where you're asking yourself, *Is this really enough?* And if you are, that's okay. It's often a sign that your values are evolving, urging you to realign with what truly matters now. To support the work you've already done from the previous chapters, we'll go a step further and consider what is really motivating you right now.

WHAT'S REALLY DRIVING YOU?

Motivation is a powerful force – it's what gets you up in the morning, keeps you going when things get tough and drives you towards your goals. However, have you ever paused to ask yourself, *What's really driving me?* For many high-achieving men, the answer isn't always clear. Often, your motivation is shaped by external pressures, whether it's societal expectations, family influence, or the demands of your career or business.

Without the self-awareness of what truly drives you, it's easy to coast through life on autopilot, reacting to situations rather than actively shaping your own path. If you've been chasing the traditional markers of success, then chances are your motivation has been coming from the outside, not from within. And at some point (possibly the reason you picked up this book) you may have found yourself asking, 'Why am I still not happy?' That's because the goals you've been pursuing might not reflect what you truly desire deep down, especially at this stage of your life.

I've always been drawn to profiling tools, as they're a brilliant way to gain insight into how you show up in the world. Let's be honest, if you've been in business for a while, you've probably tried most of them! Some are definitely more helpful than others, but there's something incredible about spending just a few minutes answering questions and coming away with a deeper understanding of yourself. Honestly, it still blows my mind every time.

For as long as I can remember, I've had an insatiable curiosity about what makes people tick, myself included. I've always wanted to understand not just who I am, but also how to connect with others in the most meaningful and effective ways. That drive to decode human behaviour is what led me to discover Motivational Maps®, a tool that has profoundly impacted my life. Think of it as a way to uncover clearly and accurately what's really driving you. It's like holding up a mirror to your inner self and getting a good honest look at your motivation – often in as little as 10 minutes!

I first discovered Motivational Maps in 2017 and since then, I've become a huge advocate. They're a powerful tool that give us real, concrete language around motivation, which is often so personal and hard to describe. I believe in their ability to create clarity and transform lives so deeply that a few years ago, I created an Academy to train and certify people internationally in how to use this tool so they can support and inspire people on their own journeys.

The reason I fell in love with Motivational Maps is simple: they gave me clarity about what was truly important to me at that point in my life. They helped me understand why, even though everything seemed fine on the outside, I wasn't feeling motivated or fulfilled. That insight was a game changer for me. It gave me the confidence to make some major shifts in my career and my life – decisions I probably wouldn't have made without that new understanding.

I'm excited to share how Motivational Maps can do the same for you. If you've been feeling stuck, unmotivated, or just not fully satisfied, this could be the key to understanding why. It's like a GPS for your inner world, guiding you to your core drivers and showing you whether the life you're living aligns with what you actually want.

The best part is that when you start using the language and insights from your Motivational Map, it doesn't just change how you see yourself, it changes how you connect with others. I guarantee your interactions and relationships will become more meaningful, and from my experience, that can be truly life-changing.

"If you've been chasing the traditional markers of success, chances are your motivation has been coming from the outside not from within."

THE NINE MOTIVATORS THAT DRIVE US

Motivation is one of those things that's always shifting – unlike personality, which tends to be more fixed. When we talk about motivation, we're really talking about what you value and what's important to you. As life changes, so do your priorities. Think about it: what mattered to you in your twenties is probably very different from what drives you now, right? Personality, on the other hand, is often more stable. Though, as we covered in Chapter Seven, neuroplasticity is shedding new light on this once fixed concept.

The Motivational Map breaks our drivers into nine core motivators. Each of us carries a unique blend of these motivators. There's no such thing as a good or bad motivator, nor is there a right or wrong profile. The purpose of your Motivational Map is to reveal what's most important to you right now and whether that aligns with how you're living your life. Here's a closer look at these nine motivators to help you uncover what might be fuelling your journey.

As you read through the motivators, reflect on which three might be most important to you right now and which may be least important.

Searcher – Meaning and Purpose

It's important that what you are doing is meaningful and value-adding. If you have a high 'Searcher' motivator, success isn't just about the pay cheque, it's about contributing to something greater than yourself.

Spirit – Freedom and Autonomy

If you can't stand being micromanaged and thrive when you're calling your own shots, autonomy is probably a top motivator for you. Individuals with a high 'Spirit' are entrepreneurial, crave independence and the freedom to make decisions about anything that impacts them.

Creator – Innovation and Creativity

You're driven by innovation, constantly looking for new ideas and solving problems. You love change and routine doesn't sit well with you. You're probably great at big blue-sky thinking but get bored with the long-term execution of your ideas.

Builder – Material Success and Wealth

You measure success by tangible results – whether that's building a business empire or becoming a Global CEO. You want an 'above average' standard of living, so achieving material success and growing your assets are important to you.

Director – Control and Influence

You love being in charge, making decisions and leading others. Control and authority motivate you to keep climbing to the top, whether in your career or personal life.

Expert – Mastery and Knowledge

For you, success is about becoming the go-to person in your field. You're driven by the pursuit of knowledge and mastery, you like detail and set high standards for yourself.

Star – Recognition and Praise

Some of us thrive on being seen. If you enjoy personal recognition for your achievements and the validation of others, the 'Star' motivator is at play. You are probably most at home in the spotlight.

Friend – Connection and Belonging

If meaningful relationships are your top priority, you're likely motivated by the 'Friend' motivator. Success for you is about creating strong bonds and feeling a sense of belonging in your personal and professional life.

Defender – Security and Stability

You value security and stability above all else. Success means creating a safe and predictable environment where you can feel in control of your future. Process and procedure are one of the things that enable this for you.

UNDERSTANDING YOUR MOTIVATORS AND WHAT TO LEARN FROM THEM

You can definitely take a guess at what your motivators are, but the only real way to know for sure is by taking the Motivational Map questionnaire. It's a simple process that gives you a clear, accurate snapshot of what's driving you right now. You can access your own Motivational Map here: cassandraandrews.com/unlearning

Once you've got your Motivational Map, it offers a huge amount of valuable insight. Here are five key things it will help you understand:

1. **How fired up you are right now:** This part should really speak to you as a high-achieving man, especially if you're into numbers! One key stat the Map gives is your current level of motivation as a percentage – are you 20%, 56%, 89% motivated?

    It also breaks it down by motivator, showing how fulfilled you are in each area, helping you see where motivation might need a boost. That's why I love the Map; it's not just guesswork, it's real numbers based on your current feelings, giving you the clarity to decide if there's anything you want to adjust or improve.

2. **What's firing you up:** Your Map will show if there are certain motivators that are incredibly important to you at this point in your life. These high spikes could highlight the things that are front and centre for you. Becoming aware of what they are ensures you can actively feed and nourish them.

3. **What's not firing you up:** It also highlights the things that just aren't important to you right now. What's fascinating about this is how it can explain why certain people or situations might irritate you.

4. **What you're not seeing:** Here's where the Map really works its magic: making the invisible, visible. If something scores high on your Map, it's almost guaranteed that your behaviour reflects it, even if you're not fully aware of it.

    This is a great opportunity to think about how others might see you and to ask for feedback. If you're up for it, this is a perfect time to revisit the Johari Window exercise from Chapter Two.

5. **Internal conflict:** This is one of the most eye-opening parts of the Motivational Map and a big focus when I work with clients. Some motivators naturally conflict with each other. For example, you may crave freedom (Spirit), but at the same time, you want control (Director). This can lead to a mental tug-of-war where you are constantly debating whether or not you should sell your business.

UNPACKING YOUR TOP THREE MOTIVATORS

I'd like to invite you to take a closer look at your top three motivators, whether you've already taken the Motivational Map questionnaire or are just guessing what they might be. Understanding these top drivers can provide some powerful insights into what's really steering your decisions and actions right now.

To give you an idea of how impactful this process can be, let me share how I worked through it with Andrew, as we dived deep into his motivators.

Andrew's top motivator, Spirit, which focuses on freedom and autonomy, scored a very high 37 out of 40 for importance. But in terms of fulfilment, it was only 4 out of 10. This meant that the area he valued most in his life was far from being satisfied, leaving him feeling trapped and unfulfilled.

We began by exploring what freedom really meant to Andrew. To help him reflect and gain clarity, I asked him a series of questions to uncover the deeper meaning behind this motivator:

What does freedom mean to you?

For Andrew, freedom wasn't just financial independence or being his own boss; it was about having the flexibility to design his day and control his time, stepping away from rigid schedules.

What's important about freedom?

For Andrew, autonomy meant making his own decisions and living on his terms, free from others' expectations.

What's the purpose of freedom for you?

Freedom allowed Andrew to live authentically, aligning his life with what truly mattered, like family and passion projects rather than being caught up in a never-ending cycle of responsibility.

What does freedom give you?

Freedom provided peace of mind and control, helping Andrew focus on what was truly important instead of being swept along by external demands.

Is there anything you're avoiding by wanting to be free?

This was an eye-opening question for Andrew. He realised his desire for freedom partly stemmed from avoiding responsibilities and commitment, an 'away from' value, as we explored in Chapter four.

How do you feel about freedom right now?

Andrew saw freedom as vital but currently out of reach, feeling confined by his business and lifestyle, which led to frustration and a desire for change.

In short, exploring your core motivators, as Andrew did with his need for freedom, brings clarity about what truly drives you, highlights areas where your life might need more nourishment and can help you understand why you are getting stuck.

Once you've identified these areas, you can make intentional, meaningful choices, whether that's in your business, rethinking priorities or creating space for what truly matters. Realigning with your core motivators isn't just about satisfaction; it's about living in a way that genuinely reflects who you are now and what you value.

OVER TO YOU . . .

EXPLORING YOUR MOTIVATORS

Now, it's your turn. Look at your top three motivators and ask yourself the following questions, just like I did with Andrew:

- What does [insert motivator] mean to you?
- What's important about [insert motivator]?
- What's the purpose of [insert motivator] for you?
- What does [insert motivator] give you?
- Is there anything you're avoiding by wanting to be [insert motivator]?
- How do you feel about [insert motivator] right now?
- How fulfilled is this [insert motivator] out of 10? (1 being low and 10 being high)

REDEFINING SUCCESS: FROM EXTERNAL TO AUTHENTIC

As you move through life, your motivators evolve, especially around significant life events, like selling a business, children leaving home, divorce or losing a parent. These moments can serve as wake-up calls, prompting you to question what really matters. For many high-achieving men, motivators like wealth (Builder) or power (Director) often start to feel less fulfilling.

Society might tell you these are markers of success, but over time, you may start asking, 'Is this really what I want?' This shift can be unsettling, leaving you wondering why previous motivators of money or power no longer satisfy you. Many of my clients describe this feeling as a hole they can't seem to fill, where everything looks successful on the outside, but something feels off internally.

Take Andrew, for example. His motivator used to be living the high life (Builder), symbolised by a driveway full of supercars. But over time, meaning and purpose (Searcher) took priority. He'd find himself thinking, *Should I sell the Porsche?* When he recognised this shift in his motivators, everything clicked. This new awareness allowed him to align his life with what truly mattered moving forward.

THE POWER OF LETTING GO – SELLING THE PORSCHE

Many of my clients have told me that letting go of material symbols of success was incredibly liberating, marking a shift towards a more authentic life. For many, the choice to 'sell the Porsche' is less about parting with a luxury car and more about shedding the expectations and definitions of success that no longer align with who they are at this stage of life.

For Andrew, selling the Porsche symbolised this shift. Once a mark of his high-achieving lifestyle, the car no longer brought fulfilment. Instead, it felt like a reminder of who he used to be. Letting go allowed him to move forward with clarity and align with what truly mattered.

Letting go can feel like a loss initially, especially when items like the luxury car, big house or expensive watch carry emotional weight, often serving as markers of achievement and identity. Over time, though, these symbols may start to feel like anchors rather than accomplishments.

Andrew's story is familiar. One client sold his sprawling home, which had become more of a drain than a joy, freeing him to focus on passions and relationships. Another left a high-stress corporate job with all the trappings of success, only to find true freedom by downsizing and pursuing a purpose-driven business.

In each case, letting go wasn't about diminishing success; it was about redefining it. Releasing these burdens allowed them to embrace a life that felt more aligned with their true values and current priorities.

REFLECTING ON WHAT YOU'RE HOLDING ON TO

The metaphor of 'selling the Porsche' can apply to many areas of life. It's not just about a car; it could be a high-stress job, a lifestyle that no longer fits or relationships that don't serve you. The real question is . . .

"What are you holding onto that represents who you used to be, but not who you are now?"

Our brain clings to what's familiar for safety. Often, we hold onto things out of habit or fear of losing part of our identity. Yet over time, these things can become burdens instead of sources of fulfilment. Take a moment to reflect on what material possessions, habits or commitments you're holding onto that may no longer serve you.

These questions may help with your reflection:

- **Does your current lifestyle reflect the person you are now, or the person you used to be?**
- **Is there something in your life that feels more like a burden than a blessing?**
- **What would it feel like to let go of that thing or commitment?**

Letting go can be challenging but it's necessary for growth. Shedding what no longer aligns with your values opens space both mentally and physically for what truly matters. Simplifying doesn't mean giving up everything; it means reassessing what truly matters now and making choices that reflect your values. For many, this involves releasing outward markers of success to embrace a lifestyle that feels lighter, more meaningful and connected.

When Andrew decided to sell the Porsche, it wasn't about finances or appreciation for the car; it was about aligning his life with his evolving values. By letting it go, he released the need to meet external expectations, focusing instead on what brought true fulfilment: relationships, passions and personal growth.

OVER TO YOU . . .

YOUR MOTIVATIONAL ACTION PLAN

Now you've explored what's actually motivating you in your life right now, it's time to create an action plan. Here are a few practical steps to help you put it together:

STEP ONE.

Get clarity: Create some time for deep reflection. Life moves fast, but without pausing, you'll stay on autopilot. Ask yourself:

- What motivators are driving me now? (Either use the real thing or your guess from earlier.)
- Am I fulfilled in these areas?
- Is there a disconnect between what I value most and how I'm living my life?
- Take your time with this; journal, walk or sit quietly to uncover insights. The intention is to see what's really going on for you right now.

STEP TWO.

Get focused: Now that you know where you need to focus, decide on one or two areas where you can make small, intentional shifts. For example:

- If Spirit (freedom) drives you but you feel restricted, reassess your schedule, delegate or explore stepping back to gain flexibility.
- If Searcher (purpose) is key, add depth by focusing on inspiring projects, supporting meaningful causes or pursuing roles like a Trustee or NED.

- If Friend (belonging) matters but you feel isolated, make time for family, friends and like-minded peers. Join mastermind groups or networks for deeper connections.

STEP THREE.

Bring others into the conversation: Discuss your motivators, areas of unfulfillment and the changes you're considering with a trusted partner, friend or coach because it can offer fresh perspectives and accountability.

If you're in a relationship, explore your partner's motivators too; it really can deepen understanding and support.

STEP FOUR.

Keep checking in: Motivators change over time. Life events and personal growth can change what drives you, so check in regularly with what's going on for you. Perhaps create some time every few months to reflect on your motivators. Do any feel in conflict with each other (part of you wants one thing and part of you wants another?) Do they feel nourished and satisfied?

Whether you take the Motivational Map® questionnaire or simply reflect and make an educated guess, revisiting your motivators annually or during big life changes helps you stay in tune with what truly drives you.

YOUR UNLEARNING

Here's a summary of some of unlearning in this chapter:

1. **Unlearn the belief that everyone is driven by the same things:** We each have a unique blend of nine core motivators.
2. **Unlearn assumptions about what drives you:** Use tools like Motivational Maps® to uncover your motivators and understand what truly fuels your life.
3. **Unlearn the idea that motivation is fixed:** Motivation changes over time, reflecting shifts in your values and life stage.
4. **Unlearn society's markers of success:** Status, wealth and recognition are often seen as success, but these external motivators may potentially no longer fulfil you. Reassess what genuinely brings satisfaction.
5. **Unlearn the idea that all motivators align:** Internal conflict is natural; motivators can pull you in different directions, like craving both freedom and control. Recognising these tensions helps you navigate choices with greater awareness and balance.

CHAPTER SIX

PULL YOURSELF TOGETHER, LAD

Andrew sat on the edge of his bed, his hands resting on his knees, staring at the floor. His head was still buzzing from the argument he'd just had with his daughter. The words replayed in his mind, each one carrying an edge of anger and frustration he hadn't meant to reveal. It wasn't the first time he'd felt his temper rise like that, or the guilt that followed, lingering like a dull ache.

He took a deep breath, feeling that familiar tightness in his throat. And then, almost on cue, he heard his father's voice echoing in his mind: 'Come on, Andrew. Big boys don't cry. Toughen up, son.' Those words had been his guide for as long as he could remember, a constant reminder that emotions were best left unspoken, buried. But tonight, as he sat alone, the weight of it all, the years of silence, of bottled-up frustration and sadness, pressed down on him like a lead weight.

In this chapter, we're going to explore that moment when the old armour starts to feel too heavy to keep wearing, when you realise that bottling up emotions isn't strength, it's survival. Like Andrew, maybe you're beginning to see that the same walls that kept you safe also keep you disconnected. Together, we'll uncover how to transform that inner tension into emotional awareness, turning vulnerability into a tool for real connection and resilience. It's time to redefine what strength truly looks like.

EMOTIONS UNCOVERED

Emotions aren't automatic reactions, they're shaped by your brain based on what's happening around you, your past experiences and the beliefs you hold. As Lisa Feldman Barrett explains in *How Emotions Are Made*, emotions are constructed in real-time. Your brain combines what it's taking in from the environment with memories of how you've reacted before to create your current emotional experience.

Think of your brain as a prediction machine, constantly using past experiences to anticipate what's likely to happen. Imagine you're in a tense business meeting. If you've been criticised in similar situations before, your brain predicts the same outcome and triggers anxiety or defensiveness, even if nothing threatening is happening right now. Your brain reacts not just to the present, but to its expectations based on the past.

Your emotions are shaped by years of experiences and deeply ingrained beliefs. For example, if you grew up in an environment where anger wasn't acceptable, your brain likely learned to suppress that emotion. As a result, you may find yourself pushing down frustration without even realising it, only for it to build up and manifest in more harmful ways later.

The good news? You have more control over your emotions than you think. Once you become aware of the patterns shaping your emotional responses, you can question them, asking yourself, *Is this emotional response based on the present, or on something from the past? Does this reaction still serve me?* By developing this level of awareness, you can start rewiring your emotional responses. Instead of being controlled by your emotions, you can use them as tools for growth and self-awareness.

"Emotions aren't good or bad. It's the meaning you attach to them that gives them power."

GOOD AND BAD EMOTIONS

In much of the work I do with clients, we focus on reshaping their emotional responses. Many have spent years suppressing emotions to stay in control, whether in business or personal life. While emotions are real, they don't always represent the full picture. They're signals from your brain, helping you make sense of the world, but not necessarily giving you all the facts.

Take anger, for instance. In business, you might see anger as a threat to professionalism, something to be buried. But what if you reframed it? Anger could be a signal that something is out of balance, a boundary has been crossed, or something needs attention. By shifting the story you attach to anger, you can use it constructively to address issues rather than suppress it until it overwhelms you.

When you stop labelling emotions as bad and instead view them as valuable information, you can approach them with curiosity and learn from them. So instead of reacting impulsively or suppressing what you feel, you can pause and ask, *What's this emotion telling me? What needs my attention right now?*

YOUR 90-SECOND EMOTION

Here's something powerful: according to Harvard neuroscientist Dr Jill Bolte Taylor, an emotional reaction physically lasts only 90 seconds in the body. After that, it's the story you attach to it that keeps the emotion alive.

This means that for 90 seconds, you can observe the reaction in your body, feel it, and then let it fade. If the feeling persists beyond that, it's due to the thoughts you're engaging with that keep re-triggering the emotional response.

"When a person has a reaction to something in their environment, there's a 90-second chemical process that happens in the body; after that, any remaining emotional response is just the person choosing to stay in that emotional loop."

As psychologist Nicole LePera states in her brilliant book *How to do the Work*, emotions rarely stay purely physical for us. Instead, we often spin stories and ruminate. For example, say you have a disagreement with your wife; you feel a wave of frustration, but instead of letting it pass, your mind replays old conflicts like, *She never listens to me* or *I'm always unappreciated*. By holding onto the narrative, we hold onto the emotion, sometimes much longer than necessary.

When we don't allow emotions to fully process, they can become trapped in the body, impacting the nervous system and leaving us in a chronic state of stress. Many high-achieving men experience this without realising it, with the pressures of constant hustle and unprocessed feelings pushing their body and mind into overdrive, leading to burnout and disconnection.

The power lies in recognising that emotions are temporary. After 90 seconds, you have a choice. Practise asking reflective questions and dig into your patterns, but also remember that some days will feel overwhelming and that's okay. Practise compassion; self-forgiveness is as vital as self-awareness. It's not about being perfect; it's about being human. That's where your true strength lies.

WHEN PHYSIO DOESN'T WORK

The Western world has traditionally viewed the mind and body as separate entities, often treating physical symptoms while overlooking emotional roots. In contrast, the NLP presupposition 'the mind and body are one' aligns more closely with Eastern philosophies, which view the mind and body as inseparable. Eastern practices like meditation and yoga are designed to harmonise emotional and physical health, recognising that unprocessed emotions can manifest as physical tension or illness.

Advances in psychology and medicine increasingly acknowledge that emotions profoundly influence physical health. As Dr Gabor Maté explains in *When the Body Says No*, 'The body is a barometer of the mind.' Unresolved emotional stress often manifests physically, contributing to chronic pain, illness or fatigue.

I imagine that, like so many high-achieving men, you've been taught to push through discomfort, whether it's a stiff neck, back pain or those relentless headaches. The usual answer? Physio, medication or other treatments to fix the issue. But I've learned, both through my own experiences and by working with clients, that unresolved emotions can hide behind these physical symptoms.

For years, I had persistent and at times debilitating shoulder pain that no amount of medical intervention could resolve. It wasn't until I started looking deeper, exploring the emotions around a business I had sold (something I'd been carrying shame and a sense of failure over) that the pain began to shift. Once I allowed myself to confront and release those emotions, the pain began to ease. This personal experience strengthened my belief in the mind-body connection, something that might sound out there at first, but trust me, it's real.

This is supported by Bessel van der Kolk who writes in *The Body Keeps the Score*:

'The body keeps the score of emotional experiences, particularly those we haven't processed or released. When you suppress emotions like stress, anger, or sadness, they don't just vanish. Instead, they can show up as chronic tension, fatigue, or pain. It's your body's way of saying, there's something emotional here that needs your attention.'

I've worked with clients who spent years treating ongoing physical pain, yet despite medication, the discomfort persisted. When we dug deeper, unresolved emotions like anger, guilt or anxiety were often the underlying cause. Just like the body holds onto physical scars, it holds onto emotional scar tissue too. When those emotions aren't addressed, the pain doesn't just stay, it can intensify.

So next time you find yourself facing pain that won't ease, ask yourself, *What emotion am I holding onto?* Your body may be signalling that it's time to process something deeper. The pain might not just be physical, it could be emotional tension that's been building for years, waiting for release.

Believe me, you don't have to push through the pain. Sometimes, the most powerful thing you can do is stop, listen and allow yourself to heal from the inside out.

TRAPPED EMOTIONS AND DEMENTIA

We've looked at how unprocessed emotions can strain your body, but they can also take a toll on your cognitive health. If you're constantly filing away your emotions and powering through, what happens to all that emotional weight? Research is increasingly showing that trapped emotions can contribute to cognitive decline and conditions like dementia.

This topic is deeply personal for me. As I write, my wonderful stepfather, Bob, is living with advanced Alzheimer's. Watching him struggle, losing his ability to communicate, remember and even move, I can't help but wonder how years of emotional suppression and stress might have played a role in his condition.

Dementia is a broad term covering various cognitive impairments, but at its core, it's a loss that's as heartbreaking for families as it is devastating for those affected.

Talking about Bob's journey made me realise just how many clients and friends have also been touched by dementia, and yet we rarely discuss how unresolved emotions might play a role in this disease. When we carry unprocessed emotional pain, it accumulates over time, quietly impacting our mental health. The body and mind are more interconnected than we once understood; unresolved emotional stress can keep the brain in a heightened state, impairing its function over time.

Dementia isn't caused by one thing alone, but here's what's important: by processing your emotions now, you may be reducing your future risk. Addressing your emotional health today isn't just about feeling clearer or calmer, it's a form of prevention, a step towards protecting your mind as you age.

Why does this matter? Because dementia slowly robs people of their freedom, quality of life and independence, impacting families just as profoundly. Addressing your emotions is more than just a mental health practice for today; it's an investment in your wellbeing, helping you stay sharp, connected and engaged with life as you grow older. It's a choice to protect not only yourself but also the people who love you.

THE FIVE BIG EMOTIONS

Throughout life, certain emotions, like anger, sadness, fear, hurt and guilt, can leave lasting imprints, like scar tissue, shaping our responses and outlook. For many high-achieving men, these emotions are often ignored or pushed aside to maintain control. But unprocessed emotions don't disappear; they become trapped, subtly influencing everything from relationships to business decisions. Releasing these emotions isn't about losing control; it's about freeing yourself from outdated patterns.

In my practice, I use both NLP and Time Line Therapy™ (TLT) to help my clients let go of the emotional 'scar tissue' they've been carrying, often without realising it.

TLT is a therapeutic process designed to help release negative emotions and limiting beliefs rooted in the unconscious mind. These deep-seated emotions are often stored from significant past events that triggered them, whether you consciously remember them or not. What's fascinating is that these significant events may not even be from your lifetime; they could have been passed down through generations. Now, I know this can sound a little far-fetched, and many of my clients have that 'Is she serious?' look when I first explain this. But with the science of epigenetics, we see growing evidence that trauma can ripple through generations, shaping not just our beliefs and values, but also our emotional responses.

Unlike traditional talk therapy, TLT doesn't require you to relive past trauma or dwell on painful memories. Instead, it helps you gain insight into the original source of emotions like anger, sadness, fear, hurt or guilt and then gently reframe or release them.

The process is simple yet profound. You visualise your life as a timeline and mentally travel back to key moments in your past. This allows you to identify when and why a particular emotion or limiting belief first took root. Once this is understood, Time Line Therapy uses guided techniques to help you release the emotional charge attached to those moments, freeing you from their lingering effects.

The result? A deeper sense of emotional freedom and the ability to move forward without being weighed down by unresolved feelings or outdated beliefs. If this resonates with you, and you think it could be helpful, I encourage you to seek out a Master Practitioner of Time Line Therapy who can guide you through this transformative process.

Let's explore each of these five emotions, why they matter, and how releasing them can truly transform your life. You'll find journaling prompts for each emotion and I really encourage you to take some time with them. Find a quiet space, take a few deep breaths and allow yourself to explore what comes up, even if it feels uncomfortable or awkward. Remember, this is just for you, there's no need for judgement here. It's just you and your journal.

If at any point it feels overwhelming, that's okay. You can pause and ground yourself, using the exercises from Chapter Two. Be gentle with yourself; this process is about healing, not rushing.

ANGER

Anger is often the one challenging emotion men feel allowed to express, surfacing when you feel wronged or frustrated. For high achievers, anger can even feel familiar, sometimes accepted. Yet anger is a powerful signal, often indicating that a boundary has been crossed, or a need has gone unmet.

One client, a successful CEO, frequently felt bursts of anger regarding his team's performance. Initially, it seemed like simple frustration, but we uncovered a deeper root: fear of failure, linked to childhood feelings of inadequacy. Recognising this, he shifted his approach from frustration to empathy, which greatly improved his leadership.

Journal Prompts for Anger:

- What is the positive intention behind my anger? Consider how this emotion might be protecting you or pointing to an unmet need.
- When was the first time I remember feeling anger, and how was I taught to handle it? Consider how early patterns or beliefs might still influence your responses today.
- What might I need to let go of to move past this anger? Identify thoughts, beliefs or patterns that no longer serve you and imagine releasing them.

SADNESS

Sadness often arises from loss, whether it's a relationship, a career shift, or letting go of a long-held dream. For high achievers, recognising sadness can feel uncomfortable, even vulnerable. Society often equates sadness with weakness, and when you're used to maintaining an image of control, it can seem easier to push those feelings aside. But unprocessed sadness doesn't just fade away, it can turn into emotional numbness, addiction or even depression.

I worked with a client, a successful entrepreneur, who after selling his business – a strategic, financially beneficial move – was surprised to feel waves of sadness. That business was more than just a source of income; it was a part of his identity, a marker of success, a reflection of his worth. By allowing himself to grieve and reflect on what the business truly meant to him, he was able to release his sadness and find clarity for his next chapter.

Journal Prompts for Sadness:

- What is the positive intention behind my sadness? Sadness often signals a need for reflection, rest or healing – what might it be trying to draw your attention to?
- What loss have I experienced, and have I allowed myself the space to fully grieve it? Reflect on any loss you've felt in your life. What did it represent? How have you been holding onto it and what fears do you have about letting it go?
- If I stepped outside of myself and observed this sadness, what would I notice about it? Step back to see your feelings from a new perspective. What might this sadness want you to learn or understand?

FEAR

Fear is one of our most primal instincts, designed to protect us from danger. In modern life, however, it often takes subtler forms: hesitation, self-doubt, avoidance. For high achievers, fear commonly appears as the fear of failure, making the wrong decision or losing control. Society often views fear as a weakness, something to push through. Yet fear is not your enemy; it's a signal, a prompt that you're facing something significant. Learning to understand and release fear is key to unlocking growth.

One client of mine faced intense fear when contemplating the end of a long-term relationship. On the surface, it was about the unknowns – finances, living arrangements and social impacts. However, as we delved deeper, the real fear emerged: abandonment and failure, rooted in childhood experiences. By recognising this, he could reframe the end of his relationship not as failure, but as an opportunity for independence and new beginnings.

Journal Prompts for Fear:

- What is the positive intention behind my fear? What might this fear be trying to prevent and is it still relevant or helpful in this moment?
- What am I imagining about the future that is fuelling this fear? Fear often stems from imagining negative outcomes. What story are you attaching to the fear? How could you reframe it?
- What am I afraid will happen if I let it go of the fear? Explore whether this fear has become a form of control or protection and what it would mean to release it.

Let's pause here and imagine Andrew. He's sitting in his office, staring at the offer to buy his business. On paper, the numbers make sense. Selling would mean financial freedom and time to focus on other areas of life. But underneath, he feels paralysed by fear. Who am I without this business? What will I do with my time? Will my relationships thrive or suffer without the structure and purpose my work has given me?

At first, these questions might feel overwhelming, but if Andrew explored the root of his fear, he might realise it wasn't just about selling the business – it was about identity, purpose and the unknown. By reframing it, he could see that this wasn't an ending, but a transition. A chance to create a life beyond the business, to strengthen his relationships, and to realign with what truly matters to him.

Fear often fixates on what you might lose, but if you lean into it, it can guide you towards what you're ready to gain. What questions is your fear raising, and how can you use them to create a future that excites and empowers you?

HURT

Hurt is such a challenging emotion to face because it touches the rawest parts of our vulnerability. Often rooted in feelings of rejection, betrayal or unmet expectations, it can be especially difficult for men who are accustomed to projecting strength. Yet hurt, like any emotion, is a signal, pointing to unresolved issues. Suppressing it only buries the pain further, creating emotional distance in relationships and even with yourself. True healing begins when you acknowledge your hurt, understand its roots and give yourself the compassion to process it.

One client struggled with lingering hurt over his distant relationship with his older children from a previous marriage. For years, he'd focused on building his business, sacrificing family time. Outwardly, he attributed the distance to his children simply growing up, but underneath, he felt rejected and unappreciated. As we explored further, he recognised his hurt stemmed from guilt for not being present during their childhood. This realisation led him to reach out with honest conversations, helping him release the emotional weight he had carried for years.

Journal Prompts for Hurt:

- What is the positive intention behind my hurt? Hurt often highlights where we feel vulnerable or where a boundary may have been crossed. What might this hurt be trying to protect or bring to your attention?
- What unmet need does this hurt reveal? Reflect on whether this hurt is pointing to a deeper desire for understanding, connection or healing.
- How has carrying this hurt shaped my relationships and decisions? Consider whether it's created emotional distance, avoidance of vulnerability, or limiting beliefs about trust. How might reframing this hurt or stepping into a resourceful state like compassion deepen your connections?

GUILT

Guilt is a deeply rooted emotion that taps into our sense of right and wrong, often weighing heavily on us. When guilt arises, especially around actions that conflict with core values, it can erode self-worth and affect how we show up in life.

I worked with a client who felt overwhelming guilt after having an affair, even though his wife didn't know. The guilt weighed on him daily, trapping him between the shame of his actions and the fear of losing his family. On the outside, he appeared to function well as a businessman, husband and father, but inside, he was emotionally disconnected.

To cope, he tried to overcompensate in his relationship, yet without addressing the root issue. Through our work, he realised his guilt wasn't just about the affair; it was tied to an internal pressure to be perfect and never make mistakes. Acknowledging this allowed him to take responsibility, begin self-forgiveness and realign his actions with his values.

Journal Prompts for Guilt:

- What is the positive intention behind my guilt? Guilt often serves as a signal for incongruence with your values. What is this guilt reminding you about what's really important to you?
- How has this guilt influenced my behaviour or decisions? Consider how it's changed the way you interact with your partner, family or even your work. Are you overcompensating, withdrawing or avoiding emotional intimacy? How might releasing this guilt allow you to engage with others more genuinely?
- What am I imagining will happen if I let go of this guilt? Do you feel guilty because you believe you should, or because it's helping you hold yourself accountable for the actions you took? How might releasing it make you feel lighter?

OVER TO YOU . . .

THE FEELINGS WHEEL

Each of these emotions – anger, sadness, fear, hurt and guilt – can feel like heavy weights, but you don't have to carry them forever. The key to emotional freedom isn't about ignoring or pushing them aside. It's about recognising them, understanding where they come from, and learning how to let them go. I know for a lot of men this can feel unfamiliar. You weren't given the tools to truly understand or articulate what you're feeling. We've already established that you were likely taught to tough it out or to get on with things, without ever being shown how to pause and ask, *What am I really feeling here?*

I understand, and it really is completely normal to feel a bit lost when it comes to emotions. Many men I work with feel the same way. You may recognise when you're frustrated, or stressed or angry, but often, there's so much more going on beneath the surface, and that's where the Feelings Wheel comes in.

We can experience so many different emotions, but most of us fall back on just a few familiar ones, like anger or stress, because that's what we know. But these emotions are often just the tip of the iceberg. Beneath anger, you might actually be feeling jealous, hurt or powerless. What you've labelled as stress, might be fear of failure, feeling overwhelmed or even loneliness. The Feelings Wheel helps you go beyond the surface and name those more specific emotions. This is important because it's been shown that the ability to accurately name our emotions can make a huge difference to how we experience them.

Below you'll find a chart I've created based on Dr Gloria Wilcox's Feelings Wheel. You can start using it to widen your emotional vocabulary and deepen your emotional awareness. Download your own copy from my website: cassandraandrews.com/unlearning

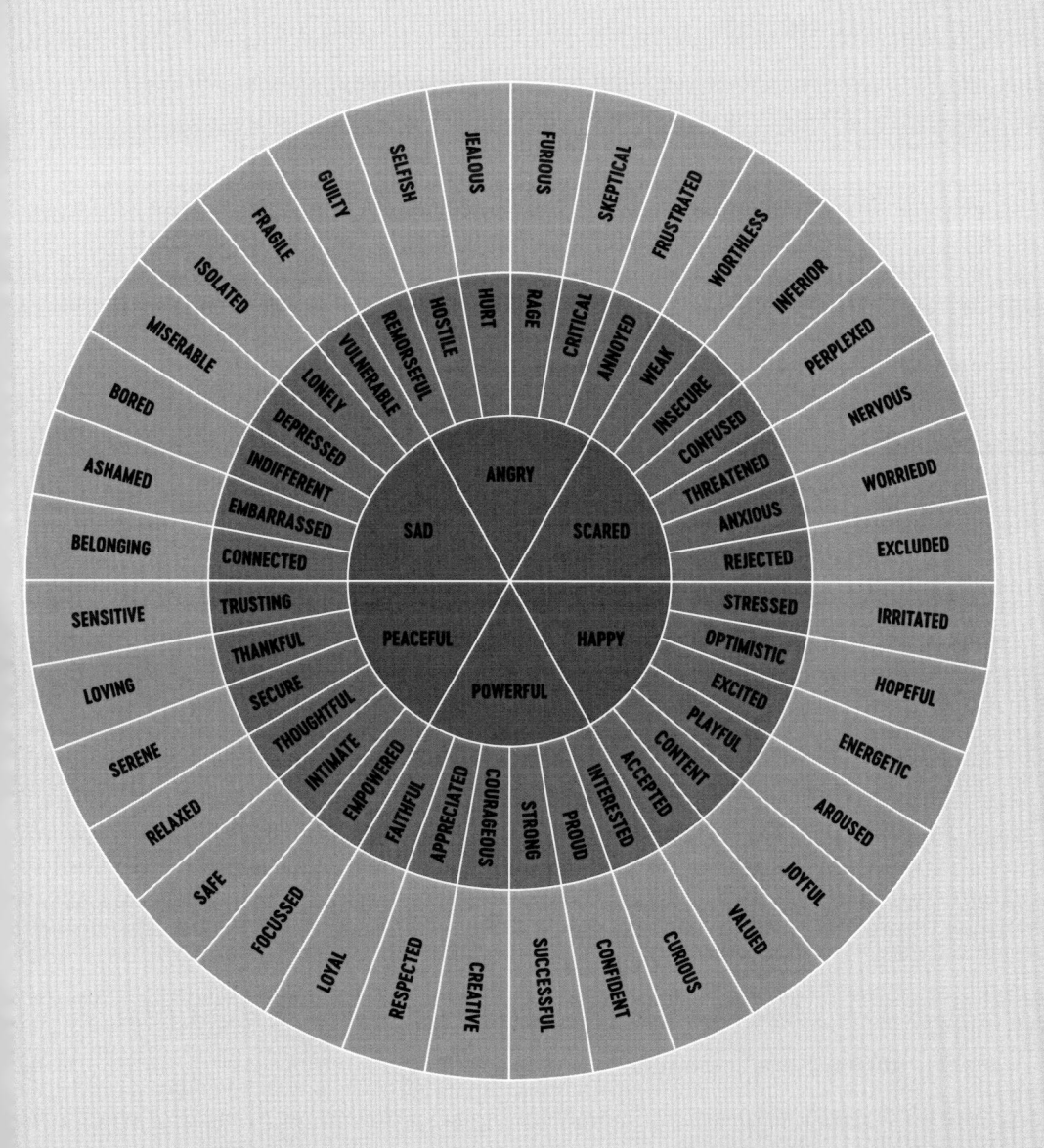

What to do

1. **Close your eyes, take a deep breath, and pause.** Notice what's happening in your body and mind. Ask yourself, 'What am I actually feeling right now?'
2. **Identify the emotion.** Start with one of the core emotions and explore outward, or simply choose an adjective that resonates. There's no right or wrong, just do what feels natural.
3. **Allow the emotion to be present without judgement.** Don't rush to 'fix' or dismiss it. Then journal about what you're experiencing, explore the feeling, its possible triggers and any deeper layers beneath it. This practice helps you understand and process what's really going on.

MASTERING EMOTIONAL BALANCE: THE POWER OF ASSOCIATION AND DISSOCIATION

In my experience, many men avoid challenging emotions because they fear being overwhelmed. But emotions, when explored with the right approach, don't have to consume you. Knowing how to shift between association and dissociation means you can 'feel safely' without losing control.

A key part of managing emotions is knowing whether you're 'associated' or 'dissociated' in a given moment. Why does this matter? Because understanding which state you're in can help you respond more effectively to what's happening. Sometimes, fully immersing in an experience is best, while other times, stepping back can provide the perspective needed. Learning to shift between the two gives you greater control over your reactions and emotions.

Association is when you're fully in the experience, seeing the world through your own eyes, seeing, hearing and feeling everything first hand. This state is valuable in relationships, allowing you to feel and empathise; however, it can be overwhelming in high-stress situations.

Dissociation on the other hand, is when you observe yourself from a distance, like watching yourself in a movie. This creates emotional detachment, which can be helpful for decision-making or to calm a racing mind at night, but if you are in a permanent state of dissociation, it can lead to disconnection from your feelings.

Moving into association – feeling your emotions fully

If you tend to intellectualise emotions, or you feel disconnected from them, moving into association will help you tune in.

1. **Find a quiet space.** Close your eyes and think of a recent situation that triggered an emotional response.
2. **Step into the memory.** Imagine seeing it through your own eyes, hearing any sounds around you, and feeling any emotions in your body.
3. **Scan for sensations.** Where do you feel it? Tightness in the chest? A knot in the stomach? Simply observe without judging.
4. **Name it.** What is the emotion? Sadness? Fear? Anger? Giving it a name reduces its intensity.

IF IT BECOMES TOO MUCH MOVE TO DISSOCIATION.

MOVING INTO DISSOCIATION – GAINING PERSPECTIVE WITHOUT BEING OVERWHELMED

If the emotion feels too intense, dissociation can give you a sense of control. It's not about avoiding the feeling but observing it without drowning in it.

1. **Imagine stepping back.** Picture yourself moving a few feet away from the scene, as if watching it from the outside.
2. **Change the visual.** In your mind, turn the image black and white or shrink it, as if it were on a distant TV screen.
3. **Shift to third person.** Instead of 'I feel anxious,' use 'He is experiencing anxiety.' This small shift reduces intensity.
4. **Ask yourself:** *What advice would I give a friend in this situation?* When you're more detached, solutions become clearer.

Andrew sits alone in his study long after the house has gone quiet. His wife is asleep, but his mind is racing. The words, 'I just don't feel close to you any more,' keep replaying in his head, stirring a deep ache in his chest. His instinct is to pour a drink, scroll through his phone, anything to distract himself. But instead, he decides to sit with the feeling.

He associates by fully stepping into the moment, noticing the tension in his jaw and the heaviness in his stomach. He allows himself to feel the sadness rather than numbing it. What's beneath this feeling? He realises it's not just about tonight's conversation – it's about months of emotional distance he hadn't wanted to acknowledge.

As the weight of the emotion builds, he shifts into dissociation –

imagining himself as an outsider observing his own situation. He pictures the scene from above, as if offering advice to a friend. From this perspective, he sees not a broken man, but someone who is hurting. This shift gives him the clarity to sit with his emotions without being consumed by them. He doesn't need to push them away, but he also doesn't have to drown in them.

Mastering this shift allows you to fully feel when it's safe and step back when it's too much. Emotions don't have to control you – you can navigate them with awareness and choice.

OVER TO YOU . . .

RECOGNISING YOUR EMOTIONAL PATTERNS

With a better understanding of your emotions and tools for managing them, it's time to put this knowledge into practice. This week-long exercise will help you uncover your daily emotional patterns and typical reactions. It takes commitment, but the emotional freedom is worth it.

STEP ONE.

Track your emotions for a week: At the end of each day for the next week, write down the key emotions you experienced. No need to record every emotion, just focus on the most significant ones, using specific words from the Feelings Wheel. Instead of just 'angry', consider if you felt 'hurt' or 'frustrated'. The more precise, the better.

STEP TWO.

Identify patterns: At the end of the week, review your entries to spot any recurring challenging emotions or triggers. Are certain people or situations repeatedly causing similar feelings? The goal is to bring awareness to these patterns so you can start understanding your emotional landscape.

STEP THREE.

Reflect on your reactions: Reflect on how you usually react to these emotions. Do you immerse yourself in them (association) or distance yourself (dissociation)? Are there moments when either strategy has helped or hindered your emotional wellbeing? Consider how you can apply emotional mastery techniques, like stepping back to gain clarity or leaning into your feelings for deeper empathy, when these emotions arise again.

Remember, this process is about unlearning old beliefs that taught you to ignore or suppress emotions. Emotions are valuable signals; lean in to them and see what you discover.

YOUR UNLEARNING

As you reflect on this chapter, here are five key things to unlearn, as you begin to reshape your relationship with your emotions:

- **Unlearn the belief that vulnerability equals weakness.** Showing emotion isn't a weakness; it takes real strength. Vulnerability enhances your masculinity, deepens connections and is essential for personal freedom.
- **Unlearn the idea that emotions are 'good' or 'bad'.** Emotions aren't positive or negative; they're signals offering insight. It's the story you attach to them that gives them power. Reframe how you view emotions to stop reacting impulsively and start learning from them.
- **Unlearn the habit of suppressing emotions to maintain control.** Suppressing emotions doesn't give you control; it keeps you in survival mode. Facing and processing emotions reduces stress, burnout and physical pain.
- **Unlearn the myth that high achievement means ignoring emotional needs.** Success doesn't require emotional isolation. Emotional awareness can actually enhance your leadership, decision-making and fulfilment.
- **Unlearn the belief that you will 'always' feel the same way about something.** An emotional reaction last 90 seconds; allow yourself to feel the emotion and then let go of any stories attached to it.

CHAPTER SEVEN

WHY DO I KEEP SEEING BLACK RANGE ROVERS?

Andrew sat at a red light, absentmindedly scrolling through his mental to-do list for the day, when a sleek black Range Rover pulled up beside him. Instinctively, he glanced over, feeling an odd sense of familiarity. Hadn't he been seeing these cars everywhere recently? Supermarket car parks, business meetings, even his neighbour's driveway. It was as if they were multiplying overnight. Ever since the idea of upgrading his own car had crossed his mind, it seemed that black Range Rovers had become his uninvited companion, popping up at every turn. He chuckled to himself, thinking, *I must be losing it.*

But as he continued on his drive, he couldn't shake the thought, Why now? Why this car? He'd never paid much attention before. Yet here they were, shadowing him everywhere, almost as if they were purposefully vying for his attention.

It wasn't that the streets had suddenly filled up with black Range Rovers; they'd always been there. What had changed was Andrew's focus. His brain had flagged this car as important, opening the floodgates for each passing one to leap into his awareness. This is the reticular activating system (RAS) at work, the brain's filter system that decides what's relevant enough to break into your conscious mind. Furthermore, it doesn't just work for cars; it's tuned to anything occupying your thoughts or concerns. For Andrew, that's more than a new car; it's keeping his finances secure, maintaining his reputation and wondering if he's somehow losing his grip on his life's achievements.

Which brings me to another filter – the voice in your head. For many high-achieving men, that inner dialogue isn't just noise; it's a relentless commentator, shaping every experience and decision, sometimes helpfully and other times mercilessly. This voice has powered your drive and accomplishments, but it's also the one that keeps whispering, Are you sure this is enough?

In this chapter, we'll look closer at that voice. Where does it come from? Why does it focus on certain things and ignore others? More importantly, how can you reshape it to work with you, rather than against you? After all, if this voice is going to narrate your life, it's worth making sure it tells the story you want to hear.

THE PROCESSES THAT SHAPE AND LIMIT YOUR SUCCESS

Imagine your brain is like a high-powered supercomputer. Every second, it's bombarded with millions of bits of data – sights, sounds, sensations and thoughts. If you were aware of everything all at once, you'd be completely overwhelmed. To cope, your brain has a system in place to filter, generalise and distort the information it processes, helping you focus on what it deems important while ignoring the rest. This system, while essential for survival, can also be a double-edged sword.

In NLP, these three processes – filtering, generalising and distorting – are recognised as fundamental to how we experience the world. They shape the way we think, act and ultimately define our reality. When left unchecked, these mental shortcuts can also trap us in outdated beliefs, limiting our potential.

- **Filtering:** Filtering is how your brain sorts through information to decide what's relevant. It acts like a personalised newsfeed, heavily influenced by your beliefs and past experiences. For example, if financial security is a top concern, your brain will focus on anything that confirms or threatens this, such as market fluctuations or risky investments. While this helps keep you alert to financial risks, it may also cause you to miss other opportunities.
- **Generalising:** Generalising can help the brain simplify all the incoming data by applying past experiences to new situations to create broad patterns or rules. However, this can often lead to stereotyping or reinforcing limiting beliefs.

    For example, if your ex-wife once criticised you for not being emotionally available, you might generalise that all relationships will fail because you're 'not good at connecting'. This belief could lead you to withdraw in future relationships, assuming they'll end the same way, even when evidence suggests otherwise.
- **Distorting:** Distortion occurs when the brain twists reality to align with existing beliefs or fears, often without conscious awareness. For instance, if your successful business hits a rough patch, instead of viewing it as a normal cycle, you might distort it as a sign of impending failure: 'This is the beginning of the end.' Even positive feedback from colleagues can be misinterpreted as insincere, reinforcing a negative outlook.

OVER TO YOU . . .

YOUR BRAIN'S FILTERS

Filtering, generalising and distorting can trap you in a cycle of stress and anxiety, reinforcing the pressure to maintain success. These mental habits often go unnoticed, shaping how you interpret situations and fuelling fears that you're always on the brink of losing what you've built – your wealth, business or identity.

Reflect for a moment: Do you filter out positive feedback because it doesn't match your belief that you need to do more? Do you generalise from one setback, assuming it signals an ongoing failure? Or do you distort neutral events to fit a fear-based narrative? Recognising these patterns is the first step to breaking free.

One way to break free from these limiting patterns is to consciously identify them. Here's a simple exercise to help you get started:

STEP ONE.

Choose a recent event: Think of a recent experience that triggered stress or self-doubt. It could be a conversation, a business decision or even just a nagging thought.

STEP TWO.

Identify the filter: What information did you focus on in that moment? Did you filter out any positive aspects? For example, were you fixated on a minor mistake, ignoring the overall success of the situation?

STEP THREE.

Observe generalisations: Ask yourself if you generalised the event. Did you draw a broad conclusion from one experience, such as, 'I'm not good at relationships' or 'People always let me down'?

STEP FOUR.

Spot the distortion: Look for any distortions. Did you blow the situation out of proportion or twist neutral feedback into something negative?

STEP FIVE.

Reframe the experience: Once you've identified some filters, generalisations and distortions, reframe the experience in a more balanced way. What would the situation look like if you weren't influenced by those limiting patterns?

The most important thing to remember is that these mental processes can be unlearned. Just like the brain can be trained to filter for fear or scarcity, it can be retrained to focus on opportunity, growth and resilience. By becoming aware of your own filtering, generalising and distorting, you can start to reshape the way you experience the world.

RAS: THE GATEKEEPER OF YOUR MIND

Imagine your brain is a security guard at the entrance to an exclusive VIP event. The crowd outside is massive, endless pieces of information, thoughts and experiences all clamouring to get in. The security guard, also known as your reticular activating system (RAS), has one job: decide what gets through the door and into your conscious mind. Here's the catch: the RAS only lets in what you've told it is important.

For example, if you're planning a holiday to Italy, your RAS will start picking up on Italian travel ads, articles and even conversations about Rome. The world hasn't changed; your RAS is simply prioritising what's now on your mind.

The RAS acts much like a personalised search engine, filtering your reality to reflect your beliefs and desires. If you're preoccupied with fears around financial security or concerns about not measuring up, your RAS will naturally seek out anything that seems to validate these anxieties. This can create a feedback loop where even small setbacks feel like proof that you're falling short. By consciously redirecting your focus to positive goals and intentions, you can train the RAS to notice opportunities, strengths and possibilities, helping you reshape your experiences in a constructive way.

NEGATIVE THINKING: A SELF-REINFORCING CYCLE

Negative thinking can be powerful because it trains your RAS to prioritise perceived threats and failures, making them seem more frequent and significant than they are. This creates a self-reinforcing cycle, where the more you focus on setbacks, the more your brain is conditioned to expect them, regardless of reality.

This cycle fuels anxiety; for example, if you're constantly worried about financial security, your RAS will highlight every risk, making it feel as though threats are everywhere. The good news is that your RAS can be retrained to focus on positive outcomes and opportunities.

Here are some practical steps to start:

1. **Focus on positives:** Each day, reflect on small successes to help your RAS prioritise positive outcomes.
2. **Visualise success:** Imagine the outcomes you want, aligning your RAS with those goals.
3. **Practise gratitude:** A daily gratitude habit shifts focus from threats to positive aspects of your life.

By intentionally redirecting your focus, you can train your RAS to notice growth and opportunities instead of fear and failure. Remember, what you focus on expands – choose wisely.

Now that we've covered how the RAS filters based on your focus, let's explore the internal 'song on repeat', the negative thoughts and phrases that reinforce a scarcity mindset.

WHAT'S YOUR SONG ON REPEAT?

Imagine your mind as a radio, constantly playing a song in the background. And no, it's not the uplifting kind, it's more like a never-ending loop of self-doubt, criticism and fear. I expect you want to know how to turn that radio off! This internal soundtrack, filled with negative language, shapes how you see yourself and the world. If you're not careful, it can trap you in a cycle of scarcity and fear, playing the same old tune day after day.

For many clients, this negative loop sounds like, *Am I still successful without the business?* or *I'm not enough*. These thoughts aren't just fleeting; they're deeply ingrained narratives that subtly guide your actions, emotions and beliefs. Over time, this internal language can become so habitual that you barely notice it, yet it holds immense power in shaping your life.

NEGATIVE BIAS: A SURVIVAL MECHANISM GONE ROGUE

To get a handle on why this happens, let's take a quick step back and look at how we're wired. Your brain comes with a built-in negative bias; it's like an ancient survival tool that's been passed down through generations. Thousands of years ago, our ancestors had to be on high alert for threats like predators or dangers in the environment. Focusing on what could go wrong literally kept them alive. In modern life, however, that same bias is still there, but instead of looking out for wild animals, your brain starts focusing on perceived failures, fears and scarcity, often overlooking the opportunities and growth right in front of you.

For instance, you might dwell on that one social event where you felt out of place, completely forgetting the many times you've connected easily with others. Or maybe you catch yourself thinking, *I'm not where I should be at this stage in life*, even though you've already accomplished more than most. This negative bias amplifies those thoughts, reinforcing a scarcity mindset and training your brain to search for evidence of failure, inadequacy or risk.

CATCHING THE SONG AND CHANGING THE LYRICS

The good news is, just like a song on repeat, you can change the internal track. Start by paying attention to the language you use in your thoughts and conversations. What phrases do you repeat to yourself? Often, these include scarcity-driven thoughts like, *I'm not in the shape I used to be*, or *If I don't make smart investments, I'll lose my financial security*.

Words like should, always and never often reflect a pressure-filled mindset. Should, in particular, carries a weight of self-imposed expectation, implying you're failing to meet some invisible, often self-imposed standard. When you say, *I should spend more time with family*, it often stirs guilt rather than self-compassion, focusing on what's lacking rather than appreciating your efforts.

Try replacing should with could, to add flexibility and reduce pressure. Instead of *I should spend more time with my family*, reframe it to *I could find ways to be more present*. This opens possibilities without guilt and allows room for compassionate improvement.

Here are a few ways to start changing your language:

1. **Daily check-in:** At the end of the day, reflect on your thoughts. Did negative phrases dominate? Write them down and ask, *Is this really true, or just a belief I've accepted?*
2. **Turn scarcity into growth:** Whenever you catch yourself thinking, *I can't* or *I'm not able to*, replace it with, *I'm learning to* or *I'm working at it*. This shift encourages a growth mindset.
3. **Reframe negativity:** When a negative thought arises, challenge it. If you find yourself thinking, *I'm never going to get back into*

shape, reframe it to, *I'm making progress with every step I take.* This shift helps you focus on improvement rather than feeling stuck in the problem.

4. **Gratitude practice:** Each day, list three things you're grateful for. This simple act helps shift your focus to the positive and retrains your brain to notice abundance.

Your internal dialogue isn't just background noise, it's the script for your life. The more you become aware of the words you use, the more you can rewrite the narrative. By consciously shifting your language, you can begin to see the world through a lens of abundance and opportunity, rather than fear and scarcity. Changing your internal soundtrack isn't necessarily quick or easy, but it's one of the most powerful steps towards reshaping your reality.

MEN AND ANXIETY: THE HIDDEN STRUGGLE

Anxiety is something many of my clients have carried quietly, often until they step into my coaching room. If you're like them, I imagine that outwardly, you've built a life that looks complete, the picture of success, but inside it's a different story. Please know that I see you. Despite all you've achieved, there's an underlying tension, a persistent feeling of unease that's hard to shake. If you've felt ashamed of feeling this way, know that you're not alone – far from it.

For many men, the outward success, the carefully curated image of confidence and achievement, masks what's really going on underneath. There's often a sense of shame in admitting to anxiety. *How can I feel like this after everything I've accomplished?* you might wonder. Here's the reality: anxiety doesn't care about titles, bank balances or achievements.

Anxiety doesn't always look like panic or sleepless nights. It's often a steady undercurrent, a worry about slipping, a fear that everything you've built could crumble if you let your guard down for even a moment. Society tells men to push through and show no weakness, so you bury those feelings. But what's buried doesn't disappear; it gives anxiety more room to grow, quietly chipping away at your wellbeing.

Anxiety is often fed by cognitive distortions – mental shortcuts that twist reality and amplify worry. Here are some common ones:

- **Catastrophising:** Jumping to the worst possible outcome, even if it's unlikely. You might think, *If this deal falls through, everything will fall apart.*
- **Black-and-white thinking:** Seeing things in extremes, where you're either winning or failing. There's no room for middle ground. *If I don't nail this presentation, I'm a complete failure.*
- **Overgeneralising:** Taking one negative event and assuming it applies to everything. *Because this didn't work out, nothing ever will.*
- **Mind reading:** Assuming you know what your partner is thinking, often jumping to negative conclusions. *They're probably upset with me for not being around enough.*
- **Disqualifying the positive:** Dismissing your successes or strengths and focusing only on what went wrong. *Okay, I did well on that project, but it wasn't a big deal.*

Cognitive distortions can reinforce anxiety, tricking your brain into seeing fears as real and immediate. The good news is, once you're aware of these patterns, you can start challenging them. If you catch yourself catastrophising, pause and ask yourself, *What's the evidence for this? Is the worst-case scenario really going to happen?* By reframing your thinking, you start to loosen the grip anxiety has on your mind.

In NLP, anxiety is often described as the future imagined negatively. It's not about what's happening right now, but rather what you fear might happen. Anxiety is that lingering fear projecting worst-case scenarios into the future. It's a natural part of your survival response, designed to protect you from potential threats. And yes, anxiety is supposed to feel uncomfortable; it's your body's way of grabbing your attention, urging you to act. The issue isn't anxiety itself; it's how you respond to it.

Anxiety worsens when you allow your thoughts to spiral unchecked. Those familiar phrases start looping: *What if I lose everything? Why am I not happier?* So then your RAS kicks in, filtering your reality to match these fears, amplifying minor issues into major threats.

SO, WHAT DO YOU DO WHEN ANXIOUS THOUGHTS SURFACE?

When anxiety starts to take over, the first step is to remind yourself it's okay to feel this way. Anxiety is part of being human; it doesn't have to control you. Here are some gentle strategies to help you regain balance, calm your body and refocus your mind.

- **Calm your mind through movement:** Exercise is a powerful way to manage anxiety, helping release that built-up energy. Physical activity triggers endorphins, your brain's natural mood boosters, and can instantly reduce anxious feelings. A quick walk, a workout, or a few minutes of stretching can reset your nervous system, calm your mind and improve sleep, a key factor in managing anxiety long-term.

- **Breathe through it:** Breathing may seem simple, but it's one of the most effective tools for easing anxiety. When anxiety kicks in, take deep, measured breaths: inhale for four counts, hold for four and exhale for four. Repeating this signals to your nervous system that it's safe to relax. Extending your exhale further, such as inhaling for four and exhaling for six or eight, activates the parasympathetic system, which helps calm the body even more.

- **Reframe your inner dialogue:** Anxiety often tells a distorted story. When an anxious thought appears, pause and ask yourself, Is this thought really true? What else could be true? This reframing technique helps stop negative conclusions, giving you a more balanced perspective. Remember, your thoughts shape your reality, so why not make that reality a bit kinder?

- **Link your thoughts to your values:** Anxiety can pull you into a loop of worry. A powerful way to break this cycle is to reconnect with what really matters. Ask yourself, Is this worry aligned with my core values? If family is one of your top values, consider if constant work worries are helping you be more present with them. Grounding yourself in your values can help guide your actions by choice, not by fear.

- **Journal your way through anxiety:** Writing down anxious thoughts creates distance, allowing you to step back and see them more clearly. You might notice patterns or repeated triggers, and this awareness is key to breaking the cycle. Journaling gives your thoughts a place to go outside your mind, reducing their intensity.

CHANGING THE SONG FOR GOOD

We've spent this chapter exploring the voice in your head and hopefully, you now realise it doesn't have to stay stuck on the same old track, like a record with the needle caught in a groove. The stories you tell yourself, those anxious thoughts on repeat, can be changed.

You've already learned how your brain filters, distorts and generalises information. Add to that the RAS, which amplifies what you focus on, and it's easy to see how a feedback loop of fear and doubt can take hold. The good news is, the same processes that have kept you stuck can also be reprogrammed, which is where the brain's incredible ability to adapt – neuroplasticity – comes in.

Neuroplasticity isn't just a fancy buzzword; it's the brain's built-in superpower that enables you to rewrite old patterns and create new pathways for growth. So, what exactly is it? In simple terms, neuroplasticity is your brain's ability to grow, adapt and change at any age.

To illustrate this concept, imagine your brain as a lively city, constantly under construction, where new roads and bridges are built every time you learn something new or change a habit. No matter how old you are, your brain never stops growing and adapting. Which means the old saying 'you can't teach an old dog new tricks' is technically outdated!

Remember those anxious thoughts on repeat? Those patterns were formed over time through repetition. But repetition works both ways. When you practise healthier habits, consciously challenge distortions, and focus on gratitude or growth, you strengthen new pathways that support a more resilient, abundant mindset.

Your brain is not set in stone; it's a work in progress, ready to adapt to the life you want to create. Whether it's shifting your filters, rewiring your soundtrack, or challenging anxiety, every small step you take is carving a new, healthier path in your mind.

Neuroplasticity gives you the power to change, not just your thoughts but your reality. If you've come this far, you already know you're capable of rewriting your story, one neural pathway at a time.

YOUR UNLEARNING

As we wrap up this chapter, here are five key things to unlearn that will help you reshape your internal dialogue.

- **Unlearn what you focus on:** The RAS filters the world based on what's important to you. Start consciously directing your focus towards positive outcomes and opportunities rather than fear or doubt.
- **Unlearn the stories you tell yourself:** The voice in your head narrates your reality. If it's filled with self-criticism and scarcity thinking, it's time to unlearn those stories. Start tuning into that inner dialogue, challenge its assumption, and rewrite the narrative in a way that empowers you.
- **Unlearn the mental shortcuts:** Filtering, generalising and distorting simplify the world but can reinforce limiting beliefs. Start questioning these shortcuts to reshape your reality.
- **Unlearn the negative thinking cycle:** Fixating on worst-case scenarios trains the brain to see threats everywhere, making anxiety feel constant and real. Unlearn this by reframing negative thoughts, focusing on growth and possibility.
- **Unlearn the 'fixed' brain myth:** Your brain is adaptable, capable of growth and change at any age. Neuroplasticity allows you to reshape habits, adopt new perspectives and build a life aligned with what you want.

CHAPTER EIGHT

SHOULD I BUY ANOTHER PORSCHE?

Andrew stood in the sleek showroom, the new Porsche gleaming under the bright lights. He could almost feel the thrill of the engine roaring beneath him, the sense of freedom as he sped down an open road. However, behind the allure of horsepower and leather interiors, there was the familiar thought: Maybe this will make me feel better. He'd always joked, 'I have an addictive personality,' using it as a way to brush off his habits. And there it was again, this need for something to fill the restless void that gnawed at him when the busyness stopped.

Andrew had spent years keeping himself occupied, diving headfirst into work, always one deal, one project, one success away from feeling content. Being busy to avoid the noise in my head, he'd think to himself in quieter moments. But lately, he couldn't shake the sense that the noise was catching up with him, creeping into the edges of his carefully structured life. Standing in that showroom, he wondered if buying the car would really silence it.

What if it wasn't about the car at all? What if the desire for that new 'toy', the shiny symbol of success, wasn't really about the thrill of driving it, but about what it represented: status, validation, a way to prove that he was still at the top of his game. As he held the keys in his hand, he couldn't help but ask himself, *What do I want? Is it really about the Porsche, or is it about that hole I can't seem to fill?*

This chapter is about those moments when a luxury purchase, a new thrill or yet another goal starts to feel like the answer to a problem you can't quite name. We'll explore how dopamine and the nervous system drive these desires, the role of our inner child and the hidden benefits of secondary gains that reinforce these patterns. By understanding what truly fuels these behaviours, you'll uncover ways to make choices that offer lasting fulfilment.

THE POWER OF DOPAMINE: CHASING THE HIGH

Let's start with dopamine, the brain's reward chemical, which gives you that burst of satisfaction when you tick something off your to-do list, score a big win, or even engage in a light flirtation that offers a fleeting sense of validation and excitement. However, dopamine does far more than just reward you in those moments.

It's the feeling that builds up before the reward, the anticipation that drives you towards it. Imagine the thrill when you're just about to make that winning pitch or the electric pull of a super car, the scent of new leather and the promise of freedom. In that moment, dopamine isn't just giving you a sense of achievement; it's actively drawing you towards the next high, whispering that this might be the thing that finally makes you feel whole.

As Dr Gabor Maté says in *In the Realm of Hungry Ghosts: Close Encounters with Addiction*, 'The question is not why the addiction, but why the pain?' Many addictive or distracting behaviours aren't simply about the thrill or reward; they're ways to mask discomfort and avoid what's unresolved beneath the surface. This chase isn't necessarily about pleasure, more about the relief that comes with it. Whether it's the next high-stake deal or a demanding workout, dopamine rushes in, giving a break from the discomfort. In doing so, it momentarily soothes the pain that avoidance leaves unaddressed.

It's important to note that dopamine isn't just a chemical for the wins, it's also activated when you manage to avoid something unpleasant. The brain, ultimately wired for survival, rewards you for escaping what it sees as threats, even if those threats are emotions or memories you'd rather not revisit. It's what happens when you skip a social event you dread or bury yourself in work rather than sit with feelings of loneliness. In these moments, dopamine creates a pattern where avoidance feels like a reward. So, the next time you're on the verge of facing those tough emotions, you might find yourself instinctively reaching for a distraction, whether that's a new purchase, an intense workout, or a text to that woman who was flirting with you.

The rewards dopamine offer aren't always tied to obvious 'bad habits'; they can be felt in places that seem entirely positive or healthy. Take exercise, for instance. For many, the gym becomes more than just a workout; it's a refuge, a way to escape the noise inside. Or consider the man who's always on the move with work, never taking a breather. Beneath the surface, these pursuits may not just be about self-improvement; they might be ways of numbing, avoiding the parts of yourself that are harder to face. There's a term for this hidden benefit called 'secondary gain'; it's the silent reward that reinforces our behaviours, keeping us from addressing what lies beneath.

Imagine a man who finds himself seeking out moments of sexual attraction or flirtation, even within the bounds of a committed relationship. Each spark of attraction gives him a rush, a temporary escape from feelings of inadequacy or the weight of daily life. For a while, these moments feel like relief, a break from the disquiet he experiences when left with his own thoughts. But soon enough, the thrill fades and he's back where he started, chasing the next enticing glance or flirtatious exchange to fill the void. Over time, what once felt exciting now feels routine, so he raises the stakes, seeking more intense interactions to recapture that original high.

This is the dark side of dopamine; it keeps pushing you towards 'more', creating a cycle that's difficult to get out of, especially when the escape feels so good, even if it's fleeting. So, what's dopamine really giving you? A sense of satisfaction? Perhaps. More often, it's a temporary escape, a way to avoid the emotional work that might feel too messy or uncomfortable to face.

It's why you might feel compelled towards the next big thing, convinced it'll finally fill the void. But if the highs keep fading, it might be worth asking yourself, *What am I really running from and what would happen if I stopped to face it?* Unfortunately that hole or emptiness won't go away on its own. It'll keep showing up, nudging you every time you win, achieve a goal or buy that new thing – and, as we've explored in previous chapters, this can leave you feeling numb, empty or in physical pain.

THE AUTONOMIC NERVOUS SYSTEM

Andrew's father was a strict disciplinarian. Any mistake, whether spilling a drink, breaking a toy or even a bad grade, was met with loud scolding words and harsh punishments.

Andrew vividly remembered an incident that occurred when he was eight when he *accidentally* broke his father's prized watch whilst playing in their bedroom. He knew immediately he was in trouble. As his father's footsteps echoed down the hallway, Andrew's chest tightened, his breath grew shallow. When his father saw the broken watch, he erupted in a fit of anger, yelling at Andrew about his carelessness. Andrew stood frozen, heart pounding, unable to speak or move, bracing himself for the punishment that was coming as his father reached for his slipper.

That moment stayed with Andrew, not just emotionally but physically. As a successful businessman known for his decision-making and calmness under pressure, Andrew was still aware of how his body reacted when confronted with conflict or criticism. Despite his many accomplishments, he noticed the same reactions: his heart raced, his muscles tensed, and he found it hard to breathe, even when the immediate threat wasn't real. What Andrew didn't realise was that his nervous system had been conditioned in those early years to jump into action at the slightest sign of stress, much like it did the day of the 'watch incident'.

When Andrew began working with me, I explained to him that his body was responding to stress in the same way it had learned to during those childhood moments with his father. His nervous system had been in a state of acute distress and whilst the physical punishment might have ended years ago, the trauma remained, lingering in his body. Andrew's nervous system had become accustomed to react to stress, conflict and criticism as though they were physical threats, even when the danger wasn't real.

This brings us to the importance of understanding the autonomic nervous system (ANS), which plays a crucial role in how our bodies respond to stress. One of the key players in this system is the vagus nerve, which runs from your brainstem all the way down to your gut, like a superhighway, connecting the brain to the heart, lungs and digestive system. In fact, vagus means 'wandering' in Latin, which makes sense because it covers a lot of ground.

When functioning well, the vagus nerve acts like the brake pedal in a high-performance car, slowing you down after moments of intensity, whether that's a heated conversation, a stressful deal or a high-stakes workout.

Your nervous system can drive you towards certain behaviours, often unnoticed. This ingrained response can mean reaching for the high of busyness, pouring yourself into work or high-adrenaline pursuits to avoid discomfort. The nervous system learns that constant motion keeps tension at bay, distracting you from the quiet moments where self-doubt might surface.

Take the fight-or-flight response. Fight might look like endless work and achievements, chasing dopamine hits with each win. Flight manifests as avoidance – scrolling endlessly, chasing distractions or staying busy to sidestep discomfort.

For someone like Andrew, this high-intensity cycle feels like ambition, but is often the nervous system's way of avoiding the quiet moments that invite deeper emotions and potential discomfort. Recognising this loop is the first step to breaking free. When you see these behaviours as learned responses rather than core identity traits, you can pause, reflect and allow room for growth. It's in these still moments that your true resilience emerges, bringing clarity, insight and a sense of fulfilment that busyness alone can't provide.

This is where polyvagal theory comes into play, a concept that deepens our understanding of how the autonomic nervous system works. Developed by Dr Stephen Porges, polyvagal theory introduces the idea that the vagus nerve isn't just a simple on or off switch for the nervous system. Instead, it operates like a sophisticated thermostat with multiple settings to adjust how we react to stress, connection and safety.

The theory identifies three key states:

1. **Safe and social (ventral vagal):** Also known as the parasympathetic response. When you're in this state, you feel calm, connected and engaged. Your nervous system tells you 'We're safe,' and as a result, you're able to think clearly, focus and connect meaningfully with others. This is where you want to be for optimal performance – whether it's in the boardroom, at home or during a workout.

2. **Fight or flight (sympathetic):** This is your nervous system's response to threats, whether real or perceived. Your body gears up to handle a stressful situation, heart racing, muscles tensing, and you're ready to either confront the danger or run from it. While this response is helpful in actual emergencies, staying in this mode too long can lead to anxiety, burnout and health issues.

High achievers often live in this state without realising it, thinking that constant pressure equals success.

3. **Shutdown mode (dorsal vagal):** When the body feels overwhelmed and sees no escape from the stress, it enters a state of shutdown. You may feel emotionally numb, disconnected or frozen. This was Andrew's reaction during the 'watch incident' as he stood frozen, unable to move or speak. While this state can protect us in the short term, living here for too long can lead to depression, a sense of hopelessness and even physical exhaustion.

For Andrew, his nervous system had become used to bouncing between fight or flight and shutdown mode, especially when faced with conflict or criticism. Even though he was a successful, high-achieving adult, his body still reacted as if he were that frightened eight-year-old standing in front of his angry father. His heart raced, his breathing became shallow, and his muscles tensed up, because that's what his nervous system had learned to do under stress.

The good news is that you can consciously engage your vagus nerve and reset your nervous system. This is where practices like breathwork, meditation or even cold exposure come in. These activities stimulate the vagus nerve and signal to your body that it's okay to slow down, take a break and recover, which can be transformative to how you experience daily life.

PATTERNS ROOTED IN THE PAST

When you look closer at the deeper patterns that drive your behaviour, it's not just about the body's automatic responses to stress; there's often an emotional core that goes back even further. Behind the masks of activity and avoidance lies the voice of the inner child. A part of you that learned long ago how to survive, adapt and seek comfort. This inner child isn't a distant memory but a living part of your mind, carrying unmet needs, emotions and beliefs that still play a key role in the choices you make today.

For many men, the idea of an 'inner child' can feel unfamiliar, maybe even uncomfortable. You've likely been encouraged throughout life to value traits like strength, independence and resilience, qualities that leave little room for vulnerability. But within each of us is a younger version of ourselves, still carrying memories, unmet needs and emotions from those early years.

"If, as a child, you didn't feel fully seen, valued or safe, those experiences don't just vanish. Instead, they settle in quietly, influencing the way you handle stress, discomfort or loneliness as an adult."

Sometimes, these hidden needs or insecurities show up in ways that aren't immediately obvious, like addictive behaviours or subtle forms of avoidance. In a way, your inner child is still trying to find comfort and healing, reaching for external things to fill those gaps left unaddressed. Recognising this part of yourself isn't about weakness; it's about understanding why certain behaviours take hold and finding ways to respond that truly meet your needs.

Consider my client James, a driven and accomplished entrepreneur who felt a near-constant pull to stay busy. To him, his work was purpose; the next project, deal or goal was always just around the corner, and he believed that each achievement brought him closer to fulfilment. But as we explored the roots of this drive, James realised there was a part of him, a younger part, that had spent his childhood feeling overlooked and unimportant. He grew up surrounded by siblings who outshone him, where attention and approval were scarce. So, he learned early on that if he wanted to feel valued, he needed to stand out. As an adult, that need to be enough had become a kind of addiction to work, each accomplishment soothing his inner child's need for validation.

If this sounds familiar, it may be worth exploring what your own inner child is seeking. By tuning into this part of yourself, you might uncover why certain habits or behaviours hold such power over you. The goal isn't to erase these needs but to understand and honour them, allowing you to choose responses that go beyond temporary relief. When we see that the drive for 'more' often echoes from past unmet needs, we can start to meet them in healthier, more sustainable ways.

The voice of the inner child often speaks quietly, shaping behaviours beneath the surface, keeping you in cycles that feel familiar but prevent true healing. By taking the time to slow down and really listen, you can uncover a pathway to address these needs directly, freeing yourself from addiction, avoidance and patterns that no longer serve you.

OVER TO YOU . . .

WRITE A LETTER TO YOUR INNER CHILD

This might feel a little strange at first, but please trust that real healing can begin here. Writing a letter to your inner child – the part of you that still carries unmet needs and hopes – can reveal powerful insights into your behaviours and emotions. In this letter, you're offering compassion, understanding and a safe space for that younger self to feel seen and heard.

STEP ONE.

Find a quiet space: Choose somewhere you won't be disturbed, somewhere you feel completely safe. Take a few deep breaths to settle into a state of calm. Imagine you're about to meet the boy you once were, who still lives within you, carrying memories and feelings that still need to be heard.

STEP TWO.

Picture your inner child: Close your eyes and bring to mind an image of yourself at a young age, maybe 5, 10 or 15 – whatever feels right. You may even want to find a photo of yourself from that time, taking a moment to really look into his eyes, noticing the emotions that might be there. Allow yourself time to deeply connect with him.

STEP THREE.

Begin your letter: Address him directly, perhaps with, 'Dear young [your name at that age].' Let your thoughts flow. Here are some prompts to guide you:

- **Acknowledge him:** Let him know that you see him and that you understand he's been through a lot.
- **Offer compassion:** Let him know he's not alone and that you, the adult, are here to listen, care, support and protect him.
- **Ask what he needs:** Give him space to express any needs or wishes. Don't try to fix anything, simply listen to what this younger part of you needs to share.

STEP FOUR.

Close the letter with reassurance: End the letter by reminding him that he's safe and that you'll be there whenever he needs you.

STEP FIVE.

Take a moment to reflect: After you finish, reflect on any insights or emotions that surfaced. These insights are valuable steps towards understanding and healing.

STEP SIX.

Shift Your physical state: Stand up, stretch or take a short walk to ground yourself back in the present moment. This physical shift signals that you're changing your state and leaving the reflective space.

EXAMPLE

Dear young Andrew,

I see you there, sitting on the edge of your bed, hands clenched as you try to hold it all together. You're only eight years old, yet it feels like the weight of the world is already pressing down on you. I see you tense up when you hear his footsteps down the hall, bracing yourself for the scolding, the disappointment. You feel like you have to be perfect, to avoid mistakes at all costs, don't you?

I want you to know it's okay to feel afraid, even though you think you need to be strong. It's okay that you're worried about making a mistake because you want so much to be seen as good enough. You don't have to carry that weight on your shoulders any more. I'm here now and I promise I'm not going anywhere.

I know you've had to learn to keep busy, to distract yourself from that knot of worry that's always there in your chest. You've tried so hard to be the best, hoping that one day you'll finally feel like you're enough. But it's okay to let that go for a moment. You're just a boy, Andrew, and you're allowed to make mistakes. You're allowed to feel confused, scared and even angry. You don't need to be perfect to be loved.

What do you need right now, Andrew? What would make you feel safe?

Maybe you need someone to tell you that you're not alone, that you're more than your achievements and the things you're trying so hard to prove. Maybe you need someone to just sit with you, to tell you that it's okay to cry and that you're still enough, even when things don't go perfectly. Whatever it is, I'm here to give it to you now.

And I want you to know this: I'm proud of you. Not for what you've done, but for who you are. For that kindness, that strength and the way you keep trying. I love you just as you are, mistakes and all. You don't need to earn my love, and you don't need to carry this weight alone.

I'll be here whenever you need me, ready to remind you that you're enough, just as you are. You can let go, little by little. I'll catch you.

With all the love and understanding I have now,

Your older self,

Andrew

THE PATTERNS OF AVOIDANCE

Connecting with your inner child and offering him the compassion he may have been longing for can bring powerful emotions to the surface. Those unmet needs, the fears and the desire to feel valued and secure still play a role in your daily life. But how do these hidden voices show up? Often, it's not in obvious ways, it's in the subtle patterns of avoidance woven into your routines, those automatic behaviours you hardly question because they feel so familiar.

When your life becomes a series of back-to-back meetings, workouts, social events or late-night scrolling, it's easy to tell yourself, *I'm just busy*, or *I need this to unwind*. These behaviours can feel so normal that they're easy to justify, even when they're keeping you from the very things you need to address.

As Brené Brown says in her book *Daring Greatly*, 'We cannot selectively numb emotions.' Brown's research on vulnerability shows us that when you try to avoid or suppress uncomfortable feelings, like fear, shame or grief, you unintentionally numb the positive emotions too, such as joy, gratitude and connection. By avoiding discomfort through productivity, social media or endless achievements, you may be keeping yourself from true fulfilment. These patterns can seem harmless, even productive, but ultimately, they keep you distanced from the parts of yourself that need the most attention and healing.

These patterns of avoidance are easy to miss because they blend so seamlessly into daily life. Statements like, 'This is just what I do' or 'It's how I cope' become automatic explanations for behaviours that, in reality, are masking deeper needs or emotions. It's only by questioning them, by pausing to look beyond the surface, that you can uncover what lies underneath. Is the relentless pursuit of success truly about fulfilment, or is it a way to avoid the fear of inadequacy? Is the compulsion to work out, scroll or stay busy about feeling accomplished, or is it about escaping the stillness?

Take a moment to consider your own patterns. Where do you feel compelled to keep moving, achieving or distracting yourself? What might be waiting for you in the quiet moments if you allowed yourself to slow down?

By becoming aware of these patterns and the emotions they keep hidden, you start to give yourself permission to step off the treadmill of constant doing. This doesn't mean you stop working hard or abandon your goals; it means you begin to make space for both your ambitions and the deeper parts of yourself. In that space, you may find that what you're really seeking isn't the next achievement but a sense of wholeness and acceptance of who you are beyond the busyness.

OVER TO YOU . . .

RECOGNISING YOUR PATTERNS OF AVOIDANCE

This exercise invites you to explore the habits you turn to in moments of discomfort. Recognising these patterns with compassion, not judgement, can reveal valuable insights and help you create healthier ways of meeting your needs.

STEP ONE.

Reflect on your go-to habits: Find a quiet place, take a few deep breaths and come to a place of calm. Gently reflect on the activities you instinctively turn to when feeling stressed or uneasy – work, scrolling, looking at porn, or searching for something, anything, to fill the empty space. Honour these habits without judgement, recognising them as ways your mind has tried to offer comfort. Write down a few of these patterns, remembering that they've often developed from a need to feel safe.

STEP TWO.

Tune into what you might be avoiding: Look at each habit and gently ask, *What might I be trying to avoid?* Allow any thoughts or emotions – perhaps loneliness, inadequacy, frustration – to surface without pushing them away. They are part of your experience and deserve compassion.

If this process stirs discomfort, remember that's okay. It's natural to feel some resistance when looking inwards. As we explored in the first chapter, studies have shown that many men would rather choose physical pain, like an electric shock, than sit alone with their thoughts for even 15 minutes. Recognising and holding space for what arises is a courageous step towards living a fuller life.

STEP THREE.

Explore what you're truly seeking: For each habit, ask yourself softly, *What's the positive intention of this?* Perhaps it's comfort, relief or peace; let these needs be seen without judgement. Acknowledging them allows you to understand why these habits feel deeply rooted.

STEP FOUR.

Experiment with being present: Choose one frequent habit. The next time you feel drawn to it, pause and take a few breaths, noticing any urge to dive in. Sit with the sensations for a moment, allowing yourself to feel them fully. Discomfort may arise, and that's natural – it's part of learning a new way to respond to yourself.

STEP FIVE.

Reflect on your experience: Afterwards, take a few quiet moments to write down any thoughts or feelings that surfaced. How did it feel to pause? Did any unexpected emotions come up? Honour whatever comes up for you.

- Create resources for the future: You've taken a courageous step to unlock some of the deep-held emotion, now it's time to help you build on this. Ask yourself these questions:
- What would it feel like to let go of one habit or distraction that's no longer serving you?

- Are there new choices or small changes that might help you meet your true needs with compassion rather than avoidance?
- What's one supportive action you can take when the urge to avoid arises – perhaps a simple pause, a deep breath or a moment of reflection?

Remember, this journey isn't about dismantling every avoidance pattern overnight. Compassionate awareness is the first step to any lasting change, and even small shifts can have a profound impact over time. Each moment of curiosity, each pause to reflect, is a step towards a life that feels aligned and intentional. As you go forward, know that you have the power to create a life guided by choice, self-understanding and the courage to embrace all parts of yourself.

YOUR UNLEARNING

Reflecting on this chapter, consider these key points to help unlearn patterns of avoidance and distraction and move towards a life that feels true and grounded.

1. **Unlearn the need for constant activity:** Allow moments of stillness without reaching for work or distractions. Presence creates space for self-awareness and deeper fulfilment.
2. **Unlearn the belief that success equals contentment:** Recognise that chasing achievements often masks unmet needs. True contentment grows from meeting these needs with compassion.
3. **Unlearn the notion that avoiding discomfort protects you:** Avoidance can amplify the very feelings you wish to escape. Facing discomfort with curiosity promotes healing and self-strength.
4. **Unlearn that self-worth is tied to achievements:** Explore who you are beyond accomplishments. Self-worth beyond *what you do* brings freedom that external validation cannot.
5. **Unlearn patterns that distance you from yourself:** Take steps towards being with yourself fully. With self-compassion, let go of old patterns and discover fulfilment in who you are, not just what you achieve.

CHAPTER NINE

IT'S NOT ABOUT THE PENETRATION

Andrew felt alone. It wasn't that he was unhappy in his marriage, exactly. His wife was a good person, a loving mother and an attentive partner in all the practical ways that kept family life humming. But intimacy, the kind that makes you feel seen, valued and wanted, had faded long ago. Sex was infrequent and it hung between them like an unspoken agreement they both tiptoed around, as if pretending it didn't matter would make the frustration go away.

Andrew wasn't one to talk about his feelings, especially with his wife. For years conversations had dwindled to logistics – collecting children, what needed fixing around the house and the endless demands of daily life. Somewhere along the way, he'd become the provider, the family 'cash point', there to solve problems, foot the bills, and smooth things over. He had a place in the family, but did he have a presence?

Flirting with other women became a small way for him to reclaim a sense of self, to feel like he still mattered, like he still had something to offer beyond financial support. Those moments made him feel noticed, even if briefly. But they also left him feeling guilty and lonelier than ever before, knowing that what he truly wanted couldn't be found in fleeting encounters or casual exchanges.

He found himself lying awake at night, wondering, *Is this it? Is this all a marriage is supposed to be?*

Relationships play a vital role in shaping our lives. When healthy, they act as a solid foundation, bringing depth, meaning and connection. However, if you're like many of the men I talk to, you might have found yourself wondering why your closest relationships often feel empty or transactional. You might be feeling as though you're meeting the practical needs of your family while your own emotional needs go unseen, unmet or even unacknowledged.

As life's responsibilities grow, so do the pressures that keep true intimacy at bay. The conversations you have with your wife slip into familiar routines, focusing on what needs to be done rather than who you are, who she is and what you both need. Over time, it's all too easy to feel like roommates rather than partners, living side by side yet somehow in separate worlds. In this space, it's all too easy to feel overlooked, misunderstood or unappreciated, a feeling that so many men carry quietly, unsure of how to bridge the gap, perhaps even wondering if they should try.

Perhaps you've tried to 'fix' the problem, or maybe you've looked outside your relationship for validation. Like Andrew, you might have sought that spark of recognition in a flirtation or a compliment, something, anything, that reminded you that you still matter, that you're more than a provider.

But, as you've probably realised, it's rarely about the fleeting thrill of physical intimacy.

> **"However exciting the chase might be and however ecstatic the orgasm, it soon fades, and you realise it's not usually about the penetration at all."**

Beneath the surface, it's about something far deeper; a yearning to feel truly seen, valued and connected. It's a desire to be recognised, to feel alive in someone's eyes, to feel that your presence means something beyond the roles you play.

Here's a question worth sitting with: What if there is more than this? What if this distance isn't the end of intimacy, rather a signpost, showing you that something has shifted and inviting you to rediscover each other again?

This chapter is an invitation to explore why these feelings of isolation or distance arise and to look at what it takes to rebuild genuine, fulfilling intimacy. It's not about grand gestures or superficial fixes; it's about exploring what's going on beneath the surface, both in yourself and in your relationship. This is the deep work that can breathe life back into a connection that feels flat, bringing a sense of aliveness that goes beyond ticking the boxes of life.

REFLECTING ON YOUR OWN RELATIONSHIP

Take a moment to consider your own relationship. Do you feel truly seen by your wife, not just as a provider, a father, or a husband, but as a person with needs, desires and emotions? Has your relationship become more about obligations than connection? Has there been a quiet resignation, a feeling that maybe it's better to stay silent than to voice what's really going on inside?

These are questions that often go unasked in the busyness of life, but they're essential if you want to create a relationship that feels meaningful, alive and grounded in genuine intimacy. This chapter isn't about me telling you that everything has to be perfect or that connection is something you're failing at. Instead, it's here to guide you through a process of rediscovering what matters to you, of recognising what's missing and opening to what's possible.

THE LONELINESS BENEATH THE SURFACE

Loneliness might seem out of place in a relationship, yet it can quietly seep into even the closest bonds. In fact, not feeling seen or heard by a partner can often lead to a deeper loneliness than physical isolation ever could. For many men, this loneliness isn't something they talk about openly, yet it's a quiet feeling of discomfort that they just can't shift.

Perhaps this feeling is reinforced by your wife, when you reach out to her with small gestures and subtle signals – a comment, glance or deep sigh – that go unnoticed. These small moments, which relationship experts Drs John and Julie Gottman call 'bids for connection', are everyday attempts to feel seen and valued.

In a healthy relationship, these bids are met with warmth and curiosity. When they go unnoticed, each missed response leaves a quiet bruise. Over time, it's easy to brush these moments aside as life's demands take over – work, children, bills. Yet each unacknowledged connection slowly widens the gap between you and your partner, creating a gulf that can feel impossible to bridge.

As this emotional void grows, you may find yourself feeling like an outsider in your own home, perhaps 'parachuting into family life'. You may withdraw or become irritable, wondering if anyone even notices. Sometimes, the need to feel seen leads to seeking validation elsewhere, hoping for a spark that reminds you of who you are beyond your responsibilities. But these external fixes often fall short, leaving the underlying need unmet and deepening the loneliness.

So, what does it mean to feel truly seen and heard? It's more than simply sharing space or exchanging words. It's about feeling understood on a deeper level, valued not only as a provider but as a whole person with hopes, dreams and fears. This kind of connection requires openness, the courage to express what you need, and a willingness to create a safe space for both you and your partner to share freely.

Recognising this need is the first step towards bridging the divide. It's a shared journey that requires showing up with honesty and inviting your partner into a vulnerable space with you. When you understand why you seek validation or why you might withdraw, you can start approaching your relationship from a place of authenticity.

WHY LONELINESS FEELS SO WRONG

Loneliness feels unsettling because, as humans, we're wired to seek connection. In early societies, being alone signalled vulnerability and risk, so we evolved to feel safer within a group. While modern life has shifted, this instinct lingers. We've already discussed in previous chapters that many men would rather engage in any activity, even something uncomfortable, than spend time alone. This discomfort isn't a weakness; it's a survival instinct that, in today's world, may hold us back from real self-connection.

Many people stay in relationships because they're terrified of being alone. However, that's no reason to be in a relationship and I'm certain that if that's how you feel, you aren't bringing your best self to the relationship. Learning to be at ease with solitude can be the path that helps you bring your whole self into your relationship.

When you're comfortable with your own company, you're less likely to reach out for superficial connections or validation and more able to cultivate intimacy. What's more, you will instinctively know that whatever happens in life, you will genuinely be okay.

To truly show up for your yourself and your partner, it helps to sit with your thoughts and feelings without the need to escape. These quiet moments often bring you face to face with your truest selves – raw, unfiltered and open. So if you're ready to explore your relationship with solitude, I invite you to have a go at the exercise below.

OVER TO YOU . . .

EXPLORING RESISTANCE TO SOLITUDE

This exercise will help you notice any resistance or discomfort you might feel being alone, so in turn it can help you understand its source.

STEP ONE.

Set a timer for 10 minutes: Find a quiet space and sit in stillness, without distractions. Notice the thoughts, emotions or urges that arise as you settle into your own company.

STEP TWO.

Reflect on what comes up: If you feel restless or uneasy, try to stay present and ask yourself what's happening. Is it the silence? A feeling of emptiness? Memories or emotions you'd rather avoid?

STEP THREE.

Look for patterns: Think back to other times you've felt discomfort in solitude. Did you reach for your phone or turn on the TV? Noticing these patterns can reveal what you might be avoiding.

STEP FOUR.

Journal your reflections: Write without judgement about what surfaced. Did any emotions surprise you? Are there aspects of being alone that feel unfamiliar or even confronting?

This exercise isn't about fixing anything; it's about noticing where you might resist loneliness and getting curious about why. Being comfortable alone doesn't mean isolating yourself; it means building a solid foundation within, so you bring your whole, fulfilled self into any relationship. In this space of self-awareness, true connection with others can grow.

ATTACHMENT STYLES AND THEIR IMPACT ON RELATIONSHIPS

The need to feel seen and heard is a part of being human, as explained by attachment theory. Dr Amir Levine and Rachel S.F. Heller's book *Attached* helps us to understand how our attachment styles, formed through early experiences, shape our adult relationships.

It highlights why we experience relationships in different ways. Whether we seek closeness, withdraw when intimacy deepens, or worry about rejection, our attachment style – secure, anxious or avoidant – is rooted in our early experiences and profoundly impacts how we seek and sustain love and intimacy as adults.

SECURE ATTACHMENT

Those with a secure attachment style are comfortable with intimacy and independence. They trust that they are loved and valued, allowing them to connect openly without fear of rejection or abandonment. In a relationship, they are emotionally available, responsive and able to communicate their needs effectively.

Reflection prompt:

- How do I express my needs in my relationship?
- How do I respond when my partner seeks reassurance?

ANXIOUS ATTACHMENT

Those with an anxious attachment style crave closeness yet fear it will be taken away. They may seek reassurance often and worry about being unloved or abandoned.

Reflection prompt:

- How do I respond to tension in my relationship?
- Do I often need reassurance and how does it impact my actions?

AVOIDANT ATTACHMENT

For those with avoidant attachment, closeness may feel threatening. They may desire connection but also fear being consumed by it. They may manage loneliness by withdrawing or engaging in surface-level interactions that don't demand vulnerability.

Reflection prompt:

- How do I react when my partner needs emotional closeness?
- When do I withdraw and what triggers it?

Understanding your attachment style helps illuminate the roots of your emotional needs. When intimacy feels lacking, it's often less about physical closeness and more about the deeper connection we're wired to seek. To find out more about your own style, I'd highly recommend reading the book and doing their short questionnaire.

RECONNECTING: PRACTICAL TOOLS TO DEEPEN INTIMACY

Before implementing any of the tools to reconnect, it's important to understand how you and your partner experience love. Knowing your own needs, preferences and relationship patterns forms the foundation for deeper connection. A meaningful place to start is with Dr Gary Chapman's The Five Love Languages.

THE FIVE LOVE LANGUAGES

This framework offers a practical way to communicate love in a way that feels meaningful to each person. Dr Chapman developed the concept based on his years of experience as a marriage counsellor and his observations of couples struggling with communication and expressing love. He noticed that individuals often had different preferences when it came to giving and receiving love, and these differences could lead to misunderstanding and conflict in their relationship.

According to Gary there are five primary ways that we communicate and interpret love in relationships, and we all have a primary and sometimes secondary love language. Here's a quick overview:

- **Words of Affirmation:** For those who feel loved through words, affirmations, compliments and expressions of gratitude are impactful.
- **Quality Time:** Those who value quality time feel most connected when given undivided attention; planned dates, quiet evenings, or impromptu moments together.
- **Acts of Service:** For some, actions speak louder than words. Thoughtful gestures, like making a favourite meal or handling an errand, shows care.
- **Receiving Gifts:** Tangible reminders, whether big or small, can carry deep meaning for those who value gifts.
- **Physical Touch:** For others, touch, handholding, hugs and other gestures reinforces connection.

You can find out your preference on the five love languages website.

If you find your wife's love language is opposite to yours and you are concerned you may find it hard to give love in this way, talk about it together (don't worry, I've got you, I'll tell you how in the next section). Share with her how you were shown love as a child, which may be why it feels more difficult to you.

Ask her to help you by giving examples of things you have done that have made her feel loved. Ask her to give you a list of some of the specific ways you can show her love. For example, my primary love language is words of affirmation, so I appreciate little notes in the bed or my briefcase, being told I'm loved and more importantly why, as well as handwritten cards and letters with meaningful words.

Give her a list as well of the specific ways you like to receive love. By doing so, you will start to co-create a relationship that ensures both you and your wife feel loved and appreciated in a way that resonates with you both, building trust and intimacy and reducing misunderstanding and conflict.

But how do I tell her what I'm thinking and feeling?

Marriage is a lifelong conversation, one that will energise you, support you, amuse you and sometimes drive you crazy! The depth of your conversation really does correlate with the strength of your marriage. Which is why it's critical you find a way to share your thoughts and feelings. If you are avoiding telling your wife what you think and feel for an 'easy life', think again. By not sharing:

- You are primarily not being true to yourself.
- You are hiding parts of yourself, which means your wife doesn't know the real you.
- You are potentially feeding more unhelpful emotions – resentment,

anger, loneliness, sadness.
- Those unprocessed emotions must go somewhere and, as we've discovered, often become physical pain.
- Ultimately you look elsewhere to be seen and heard, which may mean an emotional or physical relationship with someone else.

So, I ask you to think again – to trust your wife and let her see you. The real, messy and human YOU.

When you're ready to talk, here are a few ideas to get the conversation started.

THE RELATIONSHIP CHECK-IN

Suggest a weekly / monthly check-in. It works in business, so why not in relationships? Your lives are busy, and conversations so often end up revolving around logistics, chores and children. A check-in makes quality, productive time for you as a couple.

Make a commitment to meet every week at the same time, in the same place with some simple check-in questions to guide the conversation. Of course, it should never just be a tick-box exercise, but a structured approach will help you both share your thoughts and feelings.

A relationship check-in is a structured opportunity to reconnect with your partner regularly. Think of it as time set aside for the two of you, where the focus isn't on logistics or daily tasks but on each other. This is a moment to listen, reflect and engage with your partner in a meaningful way.

Weekly and monthly check-ins help create a rhythm of connection, encouraging both of you to talk openly about your needs, concerns and desires. If you'd like some help with this, you can download my weekly and monthly guide to checking in with your partner on my website cassandraandrews.com/unlearning

WALK AND TALK

One of the simplest ways to reconnect is by taking a walk together. Walking side by side, without the direct pressure of eye contact, can create a relaxed, open atmosphere for conversation. Moving in the same direction physically often helps couples connect emotionally, making it easier to share thoughts freely, without the usual distractions.

Consider making a 'walk and talk' a regular part of your routine, perhaps weekly or as often as feels natural. Keep it relaxed and open-ended, allowing conversation to flow from daily events to deeper concerns. This small ritual can foster an ongoing dialogue, providing space for both of you to express what's on your mind whilst building a quiet sense of togetherness. You might want to ask each other questions like:

- How have things been today/this week?
- Do you feel connected to me / am I giving you enough of my time and attention?
- What can I do to support you better?

NAVIGATING CONFLICT

Conflict is a natural part of any long-term relationship, but when it's handled poorly, it can open the door to behaviours that slowly chip away at trust and intimacy. The Gottman's' Four Horsemen of the

Apocalypse – criticism, defensiveness, contempt and stonewalling – are key patterns to watch for. This may sound dramatic but the name fits.

In his book, *The Seven Principles for Making Marriage Work,* Dr. John Gottman borrows the biblical metaphor of The Four Horsemen of the Apocalypse – conquest, war, hunger and death – which signalled the end of times, to describe behaviours that represent the breakdown of connection in relationships. Criticism, defensiveness, contempt and stonewalling can erode trust and intimacy over time. Recognising them isn't about pointing fingers; it's the first step to rebuilding understanding and respect.

These behaviours don't mean your relationship is doomed. The Four Horsemen appear in every relationship to some degree. What matters is how you handle them. Couples in healthy relationships recognise and repair these patterns, turning them into opportunities for growth rather than disconnection.

- **Criticism:** Unlike constructive feedback, criticism targets the person, not the behaviour. For example, 'You're so irresponsible' instead of 'I feel frustrated when plans change.'
- **Defensiveness:** Defensiveness escalates conflict by invalidating the other's perspective. Recognising it allows you to respond openly rather than with resistance.
- **Contempt:** Contempt, often through sarcasm or disrespect, is the most harmful. Replacing contempt with respect and curiosity strengthens connection.
- **Stonewalling:** Emotional withdrawal, or stonewalling, is a way

to avoid conflict. Taking a break and returning to the conversation when both are calm can prevent this.

By learning to spot and address these behaviours early, you can transform moments of disconnection into opportunities to rebuild trust and deepen your relationship.

UNDERSTANDING YOUR MOTIVATORS IN CONFLICT

In previous chapters, we explored how Motivational Maps can offer insights into what drives you, whether it's the need for security, recognition, personal growth or independence. These core motivators shape not only how you approach life but also how you handle conflict. When these needs feel threatened in a relationship, tension can quickly escalate, even over small issues.

For instance:

- If Recognition is a key motivator, feeling overlooked or under-appreciated can be deeply frustrating. During conflict, this might show up as a desire for validation, leading to defensiveness or a need to prove your worth.
- If Security is a strong motivator, any conflict that disrupts stability, such as discussions around finances or the future could feel unsettling. This may lead you to avoid certain topics or respond anxiously, trying to fix things to regain control.
- If Autonomy is important to you, feeling restricted or controlled in a disagreement can make you feel stifled, which might lead to withdrawal or a desire to assert independence.

Recognising when these motivators influence your reactions brings greater self-awareness to conflict. This insight helps you pause and then respond thoughtfully rather than reactively. Think about a recent conflict with your partner. What were your motivators telling you? What felt important to you in that moment? Reflecting on these dynamics can offer a new perspective and reveal ways to approach future conflicts differently.

THE DRAMA TRIANGLE: BREAKING OUT OF UNHELPFUL ROLES

When my clients are sharing conversations with me about their relationship, intimate or otherwise, I often refer to Dr Stephen Karpman's, Drama Triangle because it offers insight into conflict patterns where individuals often adopt one of three roles: Victim,

DRAMA TRIANGLE

RESCUER ⟷ **PERSECUTOR**

"Let me help you"   Drama Triangle   "It's all your fault"

VICTIM

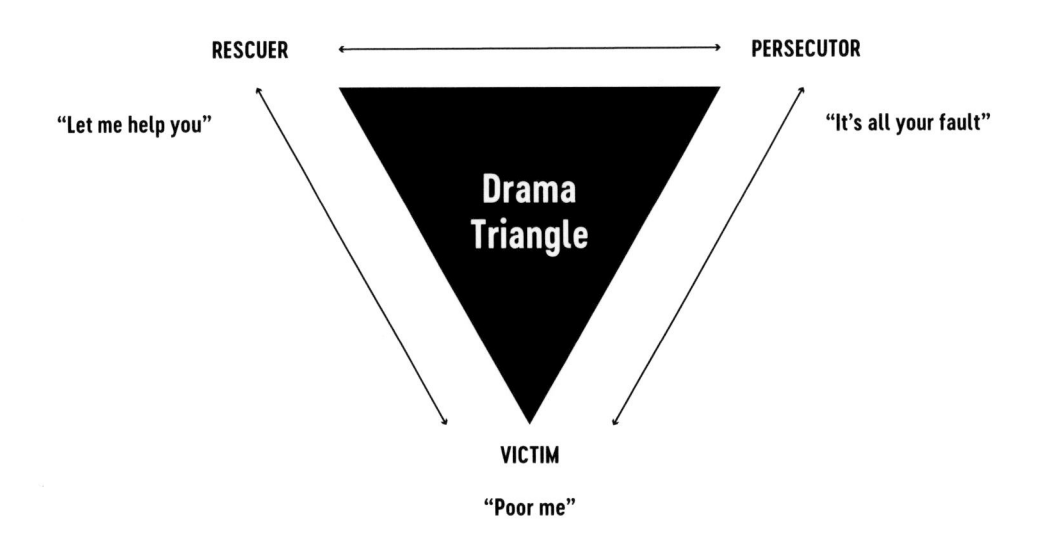

"Poor me"

Persecutor or Rescuer.

These roles can keep them stuck in unproductive cycles. Recognising these roles and your motivators can empower you to respond differently and break these cycles.

Victim: Feels powerless, misunderstood, and retreats for self-protection. This role is common when security is a top motivator, especially if stability feels threatened.

Persecutor: Takes a controlling stance, reacting by asserting authority or criticising. Those motivated by control may adopt this role if their contributions feel disregarded.

Rescuer: Steps in to fix the situation, often neglecting their own needs to maintain harmony. Motivators focused on relationships or helping others can pull people into this role, prioritising peace over personal boundaries.

These roles, driven by underlying needs, can lock couples into repeating patterns that leave each partner feeling unsatisfied. Understanding this can help you look for solutions to come off the triangle and talk adult to adult.

Reflection prompt: Consider your role in a recent conflict:

- Do you feel helpless, slipping into the Victim role when security feels at risk?
- Do you assign blame, taking on the Persecutor role when unrecognised?
- Do you become the Rescuer, setting aside your needs to maintain harmony?

Take Andrew, for example. He had been feeling increasingly distant from his wife Claire. Conflict often left him feeling trapped and misunderstood. With freedom as his top motivator, Andrew deeply valued independence and autonomy, but when disagreements arose, he often slipped into the Victim role, believing Claire's demands or criticisms were attempts to control him. Feeling powerless, he would emotionally withdraw, retreating to create the space he craved.

Claire, on the other hand, frequently adopted the Persecutor role, expressing frustration over Andrew's distance with comments like, 'You never listen to me' or 'Why can't you just be present?'. This criticism pushed Andrew further into withdrawal, intensifying the cycle. Occasionally, Andrew would shift into the Rescuer role, doing whatever he could to calm the tension and regain a sense of peace, even if it meant suppressing his own needs. This, too, left him feeling stifled and resentful.

Through recognising his tendency to fall into these roles and understanding how his motivator for freedom was driving his reactions, Andrew began to see a path out of the Drama Triangle. Instead of retreating or placating, he started to communicate his need for autonomy more openly and constructively.

For example, when Claire voiced her frustration, Andrew responded, 'I can see this is upsetting you, and I want to make sure I really listen. I just need some time to process first, can we revisit this in an hour?' This approach allowed Andrew to honour his need for space while reassuring Claire that her concerns mattered. It helped her feel acknowledged and reduced her urge to criticise or take control.

By stepping out of the triangle and engaging in adult-to-adult conversations, Andrew and Claire began to break free of their unproductive cycles. They found ways to balance Andrew's need for freedom with Claire's need for connection, creating a more supportive dynamic for both.

IDEAS FOR RESPONDING DIFFERENTLY IN CONFLICT

- **Identify your core motivator at play:** When conflict arises, pause to consider the motivator influencing your response: security, validation, autonomy, etc.
- **Shift from reactivity to curiosity:** Instead of reacting defensively, approach conflict with curiosity. Seek to understand your partner's perspective, recognising their motivators too.
- **Practise self-compassion and empathy:** Acknowledge your needs with kindness and hold space for your partner's experience to reduce tension.
- **Communicate assertively and honestly:** Be clear about what you need. For example, if autonomy is key, communicate your desire for independence without framing it as rejection.
- **Seek professional support when needed:** If conflict feels overwhelming, consider working with a therapist or coach to help identify patterns and find new approaches.

SHOULD I STAY OR SHOULD I GO?

Few questions in a relationship are as heavy as *Should I stay or should I go?* For men who've built a life around stability, providing and achieving, this question can feel like a destabilising force, stirring up anxieties about finances, family and identity. The thought of unravelling what you've built can be daunting, leaving you torn between the familiar and the unknown.

I understand the weight of this question, both from my own life and through supporting clients who've wrestled with it. It's a question that challenges you to your core, getting you to examine your values, fears and hopes.

ADDRESSING COMMON FEARS

A common fear is the financial impact. For many men, providing is deeply tied to self-worth, so the thought of separation raises concerns about supporting family and future security. There's also the question of your children's stability and the worry of judgement; you may wonder if others will see you as someone who gave up or failed.

Fear has a way of tethering you to what's familiar, even as a part of you yearns for more. It can be a powerful voice, one that quietly gives you reasons to stay in a situation that no longer feels right. Recognising this fear for what it is – a natural response to uncertainty – can help you begin to move through it. It's not about making a decision without fear; it's about finding clarity in spite of it.

BEYOND 'WAITING FOR THE RIGHT TIME'

You may have found yourself thinking, *I'll wait until the kids are older* or *I'll wait until I've secured a few more investments*. It's common to put off big decisions, hoping for a more convenient moment. But waiting can lead to greater dissatisfaction, a slow simmer that builds over time, creating resentment or a sense of stagnation.

Instead of waiting for the right time, consider what you genuinely want. What kind of relationship do you envision for yourself? What kind of partner do you want to be, and what kind of life feels true to who you are? This isn't about disregarding responsibilities; it's about realising that true fulfilment comes from aligning with what feels deeply right for you, even when it's challenging.

Taking an honest look at your values and dreams can help you find clarity. Sometimes, the answer isn't about staying or leaving but about addressing what's been left unsaid or unmet within the relationship. Other times, it's about recognising that holding on is costing you much more than letting go.

Reflection prompt: Consider your partner's perspective. Sometimes, seeing things from their side creates space for renewed compassion and a shift in how you approach the relationship.

NAVIGATING UNCERTAINTY AND DISCOMFORT

The path towards life's biggest decisions often stirs a deep, quiet discomfort, a tension between what we know and what we yearn to explore. Stepping into the unknown can feel daunting, yet it's here, in this space of uncertainty, that the possibility for real change exists. However, change can bring an undercurrent of loss, guilt and vulnerability, tempting you to delay action or retreat to what's familiar.

To help navigate these emotions, consider practices like mindfulness and journaling. Mindfulness allows you to sit with what is, rather than spiralling into fears, while journaling helps you explore doubts and hopes, giving them form on the page.

If the weight of the decision feels overwhelming, a therapist or coach can provide neutral and compassionate support, helping you untangle the complexities and gain clarity on what truly matters.

If finances are a concern, planning can be a practical and empowering step that gives you a sense of security without committing you to any immediate action. Taking the time to assess your financial landscape and understand your options isn't about making a decision to leave or stay. It's about creating space that allows you to move forward with confidence, no matter what you decide. This kind of preparation can help ease some of the 'what if' anxiety, giving you the freedom to focus on the deeper work of deciding what's right for you.

BUILDING A FULFILLING LIFE INDEPENDENTLY

Whether you choose to stay or go, one of the most powerful steps you can take is learning to be fulfilled independently. Building a life that feels meaningful on its own gives you the freedom to approach relationships from a place of fullness rather than need, to show up honestly and with integrity.

Fulfilment doesn't come from what's outside of you, it comes from knowing who you are and what brings you joy. Take time to reconnect with yourself. What are the interests, passions or goals you've left aside? Building a life that feels whole, independently of a relationship, makes it easier to approach partnership with strength and authenticity, whether that's within your current relationship or a new one.

Consider exercises that help you reconnect with your values and interests. Journaling prompts like 'What would a day of pure joy look like for me?' or 'What are three things I've always wanted to do but never made time for?'.or even remembering the activities you loved as a six-year-old can help you uncover what truly matters to you. This self-discovery process isn't about isolating yourself; it's about creating a life you love.

> **"Fulfilment doesn't come from what's outside of you, it comes from knowing who you are and what brings you joy."**

When you're comfortable on your own, you can approach relationships differently. Rather than relying on a partner to fulfil every need, you're able to show up fully, with a sense of security that comes from within. Emotional independence allows you to love without fear of loss, to give without expectation and to connect from a place of presence and self-awareness.

These steps aren't about rushing to a conclusion or making decisions without careful thought. They're about giving yourself permission to reflect on what you genuinely want, to let go of the fear of what others might think and to realise that fulfilment is within your reach, whether within your current relationship or beyond it. Whatever choice you make, know that clarity and peace are possible, even when the path forward feels uncertain.

TRUSTING YOURSELF TO CREATE A FULFILLING LIFE

Meaningful relationships grow and change, shaped by courage and honesty. As you move forward, remember that fulfilment doesn't come from perfection but from showing up authentically. Whether you choose to invest more deeply in your current relationship or walk a new path, trust that you're capable of creating a life rich in purpose and connection. Embrace this journey with self-respect and the quiet assurance that you are worthy of the love and fulfilment you seek.

YOUR UNLEARNING

As we conclude this chapter, here are five key beliefs to unlearn, ideas that may have shaped your relationships but no longer serve the deeper connection and fulfilment you're seeking.

1. **Unlearn the belief that intimacy is just physical** – True connection goes beyond physical closeness. Emotional intimacy means being valued for who you are beneath the surface.
2. **Unlearn the notion that your worth is defined by providing** – Your role is more than financial support; your identity extends beyond being a provider.
3. **Unlearn the stigma around loneliness** – Feeling lonely isn't shameful, it reveals unmet emotional needs and offers insight.
4. **Unlearn the fear that conflict will tear you apart** – When approached with openness, conflict can foster growth and clarity rather than create distance.
5. **Unlearn the idea that fulfilment must come from others** – True contentment starts within. Rather than seeking someone to *complete you*, build a life that feels meaningful to you first.

CHAPTER TEN

SHIT, I THOUGHT THIS IS WHAT I WANTED

Andrew sat alone at his kitchen table, the morning light filtering in as he stared out at his garden. Just months earlier, he had signed the papers, watched the ink dry, and metaphorically handed over the keys to the business he'd built from scratch. His hard work had paid off handsomely and by most standards, he'd won the game. But the victory felt hollow.

I'm successful; surely I shouldn't feel like this? he thought to himself, swirling his coffee absently. He had always imagined that reaching this milestone would feel freeing, fulfilling, even exhilarating. Yet, as he faced the quiet of his own home, he was met with an unexpected emptiness. Something was missing.

What Andrew, and perhaps you, may be experiencing isn't a lack of success, but a deeper call to look beyond it. Many men find themselves in this exact place, standing at the pinnacle of achievement, only to discover that it doesn't bring the fulfilment they'd expected. For years, you're sold the myth that success will automatically lead to happiness and contentment. You're encouraged to climb higher, achieve more, and accumulate symbols of status and security. Yet, for all its promises, success often fails to nourish something deeper.

I hope as we near the end of the book that you can see that true fulfilment comes not from external achievements but from connecting with what genuinely resonates within, beyond titles or accolades. Purpose is about shaping a life that feels meaningful and authentic, a life that reflects who you are at your core and what you genuinely want to bring into the world.

In this chapter, we're stepping into something profoundly transformative: crafting a vision for the life you want. This isn't about achieving another milestone or adding yet another title, it's about uncovering what makes you feel truly alive.

Imagine a life that feels not only fulfilling but also rich with purpose, where every choice you make aligns with what matters most to you. This is about shaping a future that resonates deeply, where you wake up each day feeling engaged, energised and at peace. You'll walk away with a vision that's both inspiring and deeply personal, a vision for a life that reflects your truest self and brings you the kind of fulfilment you may have thought was out of reach.

UNPACKING PURPOSE: BEYOND THE TITLES AND TROPHIES

Think of a professional footballer nearing the end of his career. For years, he's lived in the rush of packed stadiums, the pressure of every match and the exhilaration of each goal scored. His identity has been shaped around his role on the pitch, with the accolades, the wins and even the losses becoming part of who he is. But as retirement approaches, something shifts. Without the roar of the crowd and the weekly fixtures, he begins to wonder, who is he beyond the game?

Like the footballer, you may have built your identity around your roles, achievements and responsibilities. These roles have served a purpose, but they can also act as masks, defining you so narrowly that it's easy to lose sight of what truly fulfils you beyond the titles. When the final whistle blows on a chapter of life – a career milestone, the sale of a business, or even the end of an entire profession – it can leave you feeling unanchored. Often, that's because your sense of purpose has been tied to external rewards rather than something deeper within you.

Purpose, though, isn't a trophy to hang on the wall or a title to wear with pride. It's less about what the world sees and more about what resonates within you. Just as a footballer might find fulfilment in mentoring young players or supporting his community post-retirement, you too can discover a deeper sense of purpose when you shift your focus inwards. Purpose is an evolving journey, one that moves beyond the demands of the 'game' and towards something that feels more authentic and sustaining.

There's a key distinction between drive and purpose that's important here. Drive is what fuels you in the game, pushing for goals, successes and recognition. Purpose is what pulls you forward even after the game is over; it's about living in alignment with your values, not just chasing the next win. When we separate these two, we open up space for a life that isn't just productive but deeply meaningful.

CREATING YOUR VISION: THE PATH TO AN EXTRAORDINARY LIFE

I hope you've taken the time to do the exercises as you've read through this book – yes, I mean actually doing them, not just nodding along in agreement! These reflections and exercises weren't just fillers; they were designed to help you peel back the layers, uncover old beliefs, and get to the core of what truly drives you. If you haven't yet, there's still time to go back and get started!

If you're thinking, I have no idea what I want, I'd suggest you go back to the Shit List and the Wheel of Life exercises from Chapter Two. Both are fantastic resources for refining your vision and honing in on what truly matters to you. Are there beliefs or values you still need to let go of which are getting in the way? Sometimes, knowing what doesn't serve you can be the first step towards discovering what does.

Now, with all that groundwork in place, it's time to look forward. We're about to craft a vision for the life you truly want, a life that feels like it fills you up rather than one you have to keep filling. By drawing on what you've uncovered, you'll build a vision rooted in both self-awareness and authenticity, with the power to guide you towards the life that's waiting for you.

A vision grounded in NLP theory goes beyond setting intellectual goals. It uses sensory-rich language to engage both your conscious and unconscious mind, what NLP calls representational systems (or 'rep systems'). By making your vision vivid and compelling, you enlist your RAS as your ally, helping you filter in opportunities and insights aligned with your desires.

Rep systems refer to the way we each process information through our senses, primarily through visual, auditory and kinaesthetic channels. Understanding your preferred rep system is essential for creating a vision that resonates deeply, aligning with the way you naturally take in and store information.

For example, if you're more visual, incorporating vivid images and scenes into your vision will make it more powerful. If you're auditory, describing sounds and conversations can bring it to life in a way that feels real to you. To make your vision as compelling as possible, you can download a questionnaire from my website cassandraandrews.com/unlearning to discover your own rep system. This insight will help you tailor your vision to match your unique way of processing the world, allowing it to resonate on an unconscious level and truly come alive.

WHY A COMPELLING VISION MATTERS

Many people fall short of their dreams because their vision is purely intellectual. They set goals that look impressive or please others but lack emotional depth. Without that emotional connection, your unconscious mind won't respond. Your vision will remain just another task on the to-do list, rather than a true path to transformation.

We know that your RAS is the gatekeeper to your awareness. It filters out irrelevant information and allows only what's essential to reach your conscious mind. When your vision is vivid, sensory and clear, your RAS starts to bring forward resources, insights and opportunities that align with what you truly desire. You're training it to help you fill that inner space, not with empty accomplishments, but with a sense of fulfilment and authenticity.

OVER TO YOU . . .

WRITING YOUR VISION

Crafting a compelling vision means creating a future that feels like it's already alive in you, a picture so vivid that you can see, hear and feel it in your mind. This isn't about a dry list of goals; it's about creating a movie in your mind that reflects what you're reaching for at a deeper level.

Steps to create your vision:

STEP ONE.

Set a clear date and frame the vision in the present: Begin by setting a specific date (I like to do it one year from today). Write your vision as though it's already that date, using the present tense to immerse yourself in the experience. Start with, 'It's now [date], and I'm living the life I've envisioned . . .'

STEP TWO.

Let your intuition guide you: As you imagine your life, let your intuition take the lead, not just logic. Ask yourself: *What truly lights me up?* Think back to times when you felt deeply engaged and energised, those rare moments when time seemed to melt away. Include elements of this feeling in your vision; those moments hold clues to what nourishes that inner place within.

STEP THREE.

Create a rich sensory experience: How will you know when you've achieved this vision? Engage all your senses. Where are you? Who are you with? What does your world look, sound and feel like? Be specific. Instead of saying, *I have more freedom*, describe what having freedom enables you to do; perhaps it's travelling with family or investing in a passion project. This will make your vision feel real and tangible, bringing it to life for your unconscious mind.

STEP FOUR.

Stay positive and future-focused: Frame everything in a positive light. Instead of 'I'm not stressed,' say, 'I feel calm and balanced.' The unconscious mind doesn't process don't or not, so keep the focus on what you do want to feel and experience. This reinforces a positive, forward-looking mindset.

STEP FIVE.

Align your vision with your motivators: Draw on information from your Motivational Map. If you're driven by personal growth, meaningful relationships, or making a difference, make sure these are reflected in your vision. For example, if your motivator is 'Searcher' (meaning and purpose), describe how you're contributing to something bigger than yourself. This alignment with your motivators makes your vision feel congruent with who you are.

STEP SIX.

Address potential conflicts gently: As you write, notice if any part of the vision feels forced or misaligned with who you are. Sometimes, certain details might feel harder to envision. Rather than pushing through, take note of these moments, as they may reveal a deeper inner conflict or an area where you need more clarity.

STEP SEVEN.

Stretch beyond the present – create a vision that excites you: Allow your vision to stretch beyond what feels immediately possible. This isn't about setting realistic goals; it's about stepping into the life you're truly capable of living. As Richard Rohr suggests in his book *Falling Upward*, life's second half is an invitation to embrace what deeply calls to you. Let your vision reflect this openness and potential, daring to move beyond the familiar and into what feels genuinely meaningful.

STEP EIGHT.

Activate your RAS to guide you towards this future: With your vision alive on the page, trust that your RAS will start guiding you towards opportunities, ideas and people that align with this future. The beauty of your RAS is that once it knows what you're looking for, it starts filtering in the resources that bring you closer to your vision – even when you're not actively seeking them. Your role is to hold the vision clearly and trust your RAS. Believe me, it works!

Crafting your vision with purpose and intention is powerful, but it's essential that this vision not only inspires you but also aligns harmoniously with the different areas of your life and core values. Here, an NLP approach called Cartesian Coordinates helps you examine how well your vision fits within your life.

Consider these questions to uncover any hidden motivations, fears or potential conflicts surrounding your vision:

- **What will happen if I achieve this vision?**

    Imagine the positive changes this vision brings. How will achieving it impact your daily life, relationships and sense of self?

- **What won't happen if I achieve this vision?**

    Consider what you might have to leave behind; whether it's a habit, belief or aspect of your current identity.

- **What will happen if I don't achieve this vision?**

    This question can reveal what drives you towards transformation and the areas of life you're eager to change.

- **What won't happen if I don't achieve this vision?**

    This final question helps uncover secondary gain or subtle comfort in things staying the same, revealing any areas where you may need extra clarity or support.

This ecological check-in allows you to ensure that your vision is inspiring, sustainable and congruent with your life.

Creating your vision isn't just an exercise — it's an invitation to connect deeply with who you are and what you truly want.

EMBRACE YOUR VISION

Creating your vision isn't just an exercise – it's an invitation to connect deeply with who you are and what you truly want. When your vision engages both your conscious and unconscious mind, it becomes more than words on a page. It becomes a living guide, pulling you towards a life that feels authentic and fulfilling. You'll know you're on the right path when your vision fills you with both energy and peace.

When I first asked Andrew to write a vision for his life one year from now, he felt stuck. Years of chasing success had left him unsure of what he truly wanted. All he could identify were the things he didn't want: a life driven by endless achievements and external validation. This became a crucial insight, showing him what he needed to let go of and unlearn.

If you find yourself struggling with this exercise, know that you're not alone. Compassion for yourself is key. Your vision doesn't have to be crystal clear right away; it's a journey. Revisiting earlier exercises in the book can help reconnect you with your values and motivators. Like Andrew, clarity will come as you release old beliefs and open yourself to what resonates deeply.

ANDREW'S VISION

It's the 15th November 2025 and I wake up feeling an undeniable sense of calm. I glance out the window and see the early light filtering through the trees in my garden, a view I savour every morning as I sip my slowly brewed coffee. I'm aware of how grounded I feel in my body; relaxed, energised and connected to the day ahead.

Today, I'm meeting my eldest son for breakfast at our favourite café. I've noticed how our conversations have grown richer and I feel deeply connected to him in a way that goes beyond the role of parent and child. We laugh, share stories, and talk about life, knowing there's mutual respect and understanding. I feel a quiet pride, knowing I've created a relationship where my children feel they can come to me, not for solutions, but for support and genuine connection. This is the legacy I want to leave — a father who is fully present and engaged.

In my work, I've created a new rhythm that feels fulfilling. I'm mentoring up-and-coming entrepreneurs, helping them navigate challenges I once faced. I see them gaining clarity and confidence and it fills me with purpose, knowing I'm making a difference without the pressure to constantly achieve or be 'on'.

I've structured my finances in a way that allows me to pursue projects that are meaningful, rather than those that are simply profitable. I'm investing in a small wellness retreat with a friend, a place where people can come to reconnect with themselves, much like I've been learning to do. As I walk through the space, I feel a sense of pride and purpose in creating an environment that fosters growth and self-discovery.

I've cultivated relationships that feel genuine and fulfilling. I regularly meet up with close friends who challenge and inspire me. We talk about life's deeper questions, share openly about our struggles and successes and I feel a profound sense of belonging. I feel accepted and valued for who I am.

Over the last year I've embraced practices that keep me grounded. I meditate most mornings, allowing myself to reconnect with what's important. I feel a sense of peace, a quiet confidence that I'm on the right path.

I'm in excellent health. I've established routines that nourish me, running, rock climbing and time outdoors, where I feel my energy expand. My body feels strong and resilient, a reflection of the balanced life I'm creating.

In all areas of my life, I feel an alignment I hadn't experienced before. The hole I once felt, the emptiness that achievements couldn't fill has been replaced with a steady sense of purpose and fulfilment. I know I'm living according to my values, and that gives me peace. I'm excited about the life I've created, knowing it reflects the person I truly am. I'm living a life that feels expansive, purposeful and aligned with who I am.

THE ROLE OF HABITS AND DAILY RITUALS IN LIVING THE VISION

Creating a vision is only the beginning; living it is where transformation truly happens. Now that you've engaged your unconscious mind and RAS, you may start noticing surprising shifts; opportunities, ideas and connections appearing when you least expect them. This is the power of aligning your inner and outer worlds.

To bring your vision to life, it's essential to weave it into your daily routines. Think of habits as small anchors that connect your everyday actions to the extraordinary future you envision.

Here are some practical steps to start living your vision today:

- **Morning reflection:** Start your day by reconnecting with your vision. Whether it's through meditation, deep breathing or quiet reflection with your coffee, take a moment to align with your purpose. Ask yourself, *How can I live in alignment with my vision today?*
- **Journaling:** Capture insights, challenges and progress in a journal. A few minutes a day or weekly reflections can help make your vision feel real, while providing a record of your growth to revisit when you need inspiration.
- **Intentional connections:** If relationships are a key part of your vision, set a daily intention to engage more fully. Whether it's being fully present in a conversation or reaching out to someone important, meaningful connections are often built through small acts of empathy and attention.
- **Daily gratitude practice:** Practising gratitude reinforces a positive mindset and keeps you engaged with your vision. Take a moment each day to appreciate something aligned with your

vision: a conversation, a moment of clarity or simply a peaceful start to your morning.

- **Evening reflection:** Close your day by reviewing how you aligned with your vision. Notice what went well and where you can adjust, without judgement. Ask yourself, *What did I do today that reflects the life I'm working towards?* or *How did I feel aligned with my vision today?*

Living your vision doesn't mean overhauling your life overnight. It's about small, intentional steps that build momentum and create lasting change. These rituals help you stay connected to your purpose, grounding your aspirations in daily life. Over time, these consistent actions will transform your everyday reality, bringing you closer to the life you truly want.

PURPOSE CHECK-IN: STAYING ALIGNED WITH YOUR VISION

Living your vision is an ongoing journey of growth and discovery. As you progress, your sense of purpose may shift, revealing new layers of meaning. Regular reflection helps keep your vision vibrant, true and deeply personal.

Take time each month or season to pause and reconnect with what matters most. Honour your progress, explore emerging values and priorities and make gentle adjustments that bring you even closer to the life you truly want. Use these prompts to guide your reflections:

- **Am I moving towards the life I envision?** Notice any shifts in your mindset, values, or clarity around what matters most. Are there parts of your vision that now feel even more meaningful?

- **Are there areas where I feel out of sync?** Gently explore where you may feel disconnected and consider adjustments with compassion and curiosity.
- **How can I deepen my commitment to this vision?** Consider any small shifts or new practices that could strengthen your connection with your purpose.

By regularly checking in, you nurture a living relationship with your vision. Fulfilment isn't a destination but a continuous journey that evolves with you. Embrace the process, knowing every step brings you closer to a life of meaning and authenticity; a life that is both extraordinary and genuinely yours.

YOUR UNLEARNING

Here's a quick recap of the chapter. Each of these unlearning points is designed to guide you as you create a vision that truly resonates, moving you away from old patterns and towards a life that feels purposeful and fulfilling.

1. **Unlearn the belief that success guarantees fulfilment:** True fulfilment comes from inner alignment and a life guided by purpose, not just achieving external goals.
2. **Unlearn the need to define yourself by roles and status:** Purpose lives beyond titles, in the values and passions that resonate deeply within you.
3. **Unlearn the fear of imagining a bigger vision:** Dare to create a vision that feels exciting and expansive. Your vision must stretch beyond immediate goals and reflect the life you truly desire.
4. **Unlearn the habit of planning without emotional connection:** A compelling vision isn't just a checklist; it's a sensory-rich experience that engages both your conscious and unconscious mind.
5. **Unlearn the idea that your vision is fixed:** Let your vision evolve as you grow, adapting to reflect your changing priorities and insights.

CONCLUSION

YOU DON'T NEED ALL THE ANSWERS

Here we are, at the final page and yet, this doesn't feel like an ending at all, it feels like the beginning of something new.

I want to pause here and acknowledge what you've done by reading these pages. You've given yourself permission to stop, to reflect and to explore the stories and beliefs that have shaped your life up until now. That's no small thing. After having spent decades achieving, building and providing, it can feel almost unnatural to press pause and ask, what about me?

Yet here you are. You've started the work; turning inwards, questioning the narratives you've lived by and uncovering what truly matters to you. You've asked yourself the kind of questions most men avoid their entire lives: *What do I want? Is this enough?*

I truly believe in the transformational power of therapeutic coaching. In my years of working with high-achieving men, I've witnessed the extraordinary changes that happen when someone is willing to take an honest look at themselves. This book is my way of sharing some of the tools I use with my clients; tools to help you see yourself more clearly and realise there is another way, if you choose to take it.

I also believe a light must be shone both on and for men. For too long, men have navigated their inner world in silence. That silence has been normalised. But that silence has a cost.

We need men talking. Sharing their emotional journeys. Showing up not just for their families and businesses, but for themselves. It's in these conversations – in the raw, unguarded truths – that transformation begins. My hope is that through these pages, you've felt seen, heard and maybe even understood.

Bronnie Ware, in her reflections on *The Top Five Regrets of the Dying*, shared five common regrets that people express near the end of their lives:

- **'I wish I'd had the courage to live a life true to myself, not the life others expected of me.'**
- **'I wish I hadn't worked so hard.'**
- **'I wish I'd had the courage to express my feelings.'**
- **'I wish I had stayed in touch with my friends.'**
- **'I wish that I had let myself be happier.'**

When I first read these words, they stopped me in my tracks. Not because they were surprising, but because they rang so true. I've heard these same regrets in the conversations I've had with men who feel trapped by the lives they've built, unsure of how to break free.

My wish for you is that none of these regrets become yours.

You have the courage to live a life true to yourself, not the one others expect of you. You have the ability to express what you feel, without shame or fear. To reconnect with the people who matter most. To savour joy and ease instead of constantly chasing the next achievement. To redefine what success looks like for you, on your own terms.

If there's one thing I hope you'll take from this book, it's that your life is yours to write. You are not defined by the beliefs you've carried, the mistakes you've made, or the expectations others have placed on you.

You don't need all the answers. You don't need a perfect plan. You just need to take the next step. Everything you need is already within you.

So here's my invitation: Take what resonated with you from these pages and act on it. Imagine the life you'd live if you weren't afraid of what others might think. Have the conversations you've been avoiding. Pause before rushing into the next achievement. Share your story with someone who might need to hear it.

Because this isn't the end, it's your beginning. The story of your life isn't written in stone. What you do next, how you show up in your relationships, in your work and most importantly, with yourself, is yours to choose.

Take a deep breath. Honour how far you've come. And write the next chapter of your life with intention, courage and a little more ease.

Because this is your story. What will you write?

I'm rooting for you,

RESOURCES TO SUPPORT YOUR JOURNEY

Below are some tools and techniques I mention in Chapter Two (I've been waiting for you).

BREATHWORK PRACTICES

Before beginning any of these practices, take a moment to settle yourself:

- Find a comfortable place to sit or lie down where you won't be disturbed.
- Gently release tension – soften your jaw, relax your tongue, and ease the muscles in your face and shoulders.
- Choose what feels right – you can close your eyes or keep them open. Personally, I like to close my eyes to limit distractions.

Each technique serves a different purpose – choose the one that fits your energy, emotions, or situation.

4-7-8 BREATHING *(FOR RELAXATION & SLEEP)*

Best used when you're feeling anxious, overwhelmed, or struggling to switch off at night. This technique helps activate your parasympathetic nervous system, slowing your heart rate and calming your mind.

- Inhale slowly and deeply through your nose for 4 counts.
- Hold your breath for 7 counts.
- Exhale completely using a 'whoosh' sigh for 8 counts, releasing any emotions or thoughts as you do.
- Repeat the cycle for one to two minutes.
- Check in – notice how your body feels.

BOX BREATHING *(FOR FOCUS AND STRESS REDUCTION)*

Used by athletes, Navy SEALs, and high performers, this technique helps regulate your nervous system and regain control in high-pressure situations. It's great for centring yourself before an important meeting, difficult conversation, or decision.

- Inhale deeply through your nose for 4 counts.
- Hold your breath for 4 counts.
- Exhale for 4 counts.
- Hold your breath again for 4 counts.
- Repeat the cycle for one to two minutes.
- Check in – notice how your body feels.

ALTERNATE NOSTRIL BREATHING *(FOR RELAXATION AND STRESS REDUCTION)*

A powerful practice for balancing the mind and body, often used in yoga and meditation. It's especially helpful when you feel mentally foggy, overstimulated, or emotionally out of sync.

- Sit comfortably with your spine straight and shoulders relaxed. Rest your left hand on your left leg, palm facing upward.
- With your right hand, bring your index and middle fingers to the bridge of your nose, between your eyebrows.
- Let your thumb and ring finger rest gently on either side of your nose, and take a deep breath in.
- Gently close both nostrils slightly, allowing a small amount of air to pass through, and exhale fully.
- Close your right nostril with your thumb and inhale slowly through

your left nostril.
- Close your left nostril with your ring finger, holding both nostrils closed for a brief pause.
- Open your right nostril and exhale slowly through the right side, pausing briefly at the bottom of the breath.
- Inhale through your right nostril.
- Close both nostrils (thumb and ring finger).
- Open your left nostril and exhale slowly through the left side, pausing briefly at the bottom.
- Repeat for one to two minutes, or whatever feels right for you – just make sure to keep each side equal.
- Check in – notice how your body feels.

FINAL THOUGHTS

Breathwork is a simple but powerful tool – one that's always available to you, no matter where you are. Try experimenting with these techniques in different situations and notice what works best for you. The more you practise, the more instinctive it becomes.

JOURNALING

Journaling is an amazing tool for gaining clarity, processing emotions, and creating space for new insights. If you don't know where to start, download my simple 24 page guide to journaling for men.

www.cassandraandrews.com/journaling

BOOKS THAT SHAPED THIS WORK

My thinking and the ideas in this book have been shaped by a lifetime of experience, years of learning, and the work I've done with clients. These books have also played a role, offering insights that continue to influence my approach.

This book is designed to be practical – real change comes from action, not just more information. It's easy to get lost in a sea of books, but if you're looking to go deeper, these are the ones I regularly return to and recommend to clients.

ON PURPOSE, MEANING & MANHOOD

The Top Five Regrets of the Dying – Bronnie Ware (Hay House, 2019)

The Monk Who Sold His Ferrari – Robin Sharma (Thorsons, 2015)

Manhood – Steve Biddulph (Vermilion, 2015)

The Mask of Masculinity – Lewis Howes (Hay House UK, 2017)

ON THE MIND & EMOTIONS

How Emotions Are Made: The Secret Life of the Brain – Lisa Feldman Barrett (Pan, 2018)

How to Do the Work: Recognize Your Patterns, Heal from Your Past, and Create Your Self – Dr. Nicole LePera (Orion Spring, 2021)

When the Body Says No: The Cost of Hidden Stress – Dr. Gabor Maté (Vermilion, 2019)

The Body Keeps the Score: Brain, Mind, and Body in the Healing of Trauma – Bessel van der Kolk (Penguin, 2015)

Daring Greatly: How the Courage to Be Vulnerable Transforms the Way We Live, Love, Parent, and Lead – Brené Brown (Penguin Life, 2015)

In the Realm of Hungry Ghosts: Close Encounters with Addiction – Dr. Gabor Maté (Vermilion, 2018)

The Chimp Paradox: The Mind Management Programme to Help You Achieve Success, Confidence and Happiness – Prof. Steve Peters (Vermilion, 2012)

High Performance: Lessons from the Best on Becoming Your Best – Jake Humphrey & Prof. Damian Hughes (Random House, 2021)

The Wealth Money Can't Buy: The 8 Hidden Habits to Live Your Richest Life – Robin Sharma (Rider, 2024)

The High Five Habit: Take Control of Your Life with One Simple Habit – Mel Robbins (Hay House, 2021)

ON RELATIONSHIPS & CONNECTION

Eight Dates: To keep your relationship happy, thriving and lasting – John Gottman & Julie Schwartz Gottman (Penguin Life, 2019)

Attached: The New Science of Adult Attachment and How It Can Help You Find – and Keep – Love – Dr. Amir Levine & Rachel S.F. Heller (Bluebird, 2011)

The Five Love Languages: The Secret to Love That Lasts – Dr. Gary Chapman (Northfield Publishing, 2015)

The Seven-Day Love Prescription – John Gottman & Julie Schwartz Gottman (Penguin Life, 2022)

ADDITIONAL INSIGHTS

Bliss More: How to Succeed in Meditation Without Really Trying – Light Watkins (Ballantine Books, 2018)

Enough?: How Much Money Do You Need For The Rest of Your Life? – Paul D. Armson (Paul Armson, 2016)

GREAT LISTENS (PODCASTS WORTH YOUR TIME)

The High Performance Podcast – Jake Humphrey & Damian Hughes

The School of Greatness – Lewis Howes

Feel Better, Live More – Dr. Rangan Chatterjee

The Diary of a CEO – Steven Bartlett

The Mel Robbins Podcast – Mel Robbins

On Purpose with Jay Shetty

Slow Mo – Mo Gawdat

The Light Watkins Show – Light Watkins

The Huberman Lab Podcast – Dr. Andrew Huberman

WHAT'S NEXT?

You've read the book, reflected, and maybe started questioning things in ways you never have before. That's where real change begins.

So now, the question is: what will you do with what you've discovered?

Awareness is powerful, but action is what creates transformation. If you're ready to take the next step, here's where to start:

- **Get Clarity on Your Life** – Take the 'Are You Living Your Best Life?' scorecard to assess where you are and what needs to shift. Start here: www.cassandraandrews.com/scorecard
- **Understand What Drives You** – Take my Motivational Map & Feedback assessment to uncover what truly motivates you and get personalised insights to move forward. Get yours here: www.cassandraandrews.com/unlearning

> "Whatever you do, don't let this just be another book you read and forget. You don't have to have it all figured out, but you do have to start."

I WANT TO ACKNOWLEDGE YOU . . .

Mum – thank you for sharing your love of words, writing, and human psychology with me. It shaped the way I see the world and led me to this book. Your strength, passion, and unwavering belief in me mean everything. I am endlessly grateful to be your daughter.

Dad – though you may not be here in body, you are with me every day as I navigate a world dedicated to helping men. Thank you for shaping the way I see, understand, and support them. Your presence is felt in every word of this book.

Bob – my stepdad, my 'silent support.' Thank you for the quiet strength that gave me the confidence and freedom to explore who I wanted to be. For that, I am deeply grateful. Though Alzheimer's may take pieces of the present, it will never diminish the tremendous impact you've had on my life.

Tom Krykant – thank you for standing beside me. For your consistent encouragement, your honesty, and your unwavering belief in my writing. For sharing in my excitement, for holding space when I needed it, and for knowing me in a way only you do.

Trusted Readers – you know who you are, and I can't begin to thank you enough. Your time, commitment, and kindness have meant the world to me. Reading the first draft of this manuscript and offering your guidance, insights, and suggestions helped shape this book in ways I couldn't have done alone. I appreciate you more than words can say.

My Coaches – I would not be the person I am today without the wisdom, guidance, and support of those who have coached me. In particular, Jo Rayner, who helped me explore the hurt parts of myself with care and compassion, and Bevis Moynan, who guided me even deeper. You are both exceptionally gifted coaches, and I am more grateful than you will ever know. A special thank you also to Paul Ward, for opening the door to the world of coaching and showing me what was possible.

Clients – thank you for your trust, for inviting me into your world, and for sharing so openly. It is a privilege. I am in awe of your courage and curiosity to explore your inner world, and I learn from you every day.

James and Linda Sale – James, thank you for creating Motivational Maps, they have profoundly changed the trajectory of my life. Linda, as MD of the business, your generosity, support, and collaborative spirit have made all the difference. I deeply appreciate both of you and the impact you've had on my journey.

Publishing Team – thank you for bringing this book to life. Your expertise, patience, and guidance have made this journey smoother and more enjoyable than I ever imagined. A special thank you to

Sophie Elletson, Kam Bains, Daniel Prescott-Bennett, and Vickie Boff - your talent and dedication have left an indelible mark on this book, and I am truly grateful.

Simon Thomas – thank you for lending your voice to the start of this book. Your willingness to share your words, your time, and your perspective has added something truly special. I'm honoured to have your foreword open these pages, and deeply grateful for your generosity and belief in my message.

Matt Sykes – I remember the day you told me you couldn't help me any further unless I wrote the book. Well, look what that did! Your unwavering support, week after week, kept me moving forward, and this book simply wouldn't exist without you. Thank you for believing in me and pushing me when I needed it most.

Chris Reeve – thank you for your unwavering generosity and the way you quietly open doors for others. Your willingness to champion my book and share it within your world has meant more to me than I can say. Your support is thoughtful, wholehearted, and deeply appreciated.

Adam Sutton – my dear friend, you saw the coach in me before I ever did. Thank you for trusting me with your story, for showing up and doing the work, and for the joy you bring into my life. Thank you for listening, for truly seeing me, and for a connection that is rare and deeply cherished. I am so grateful for you.

Incredible Support and Business Network (AKA Street Team) – I don't know where to begin to thank my vast and extraordinary network, especially my Norfolk community, who continually support, cheerlead, and encourage me. One person who deserves a special mention is Mark Juniper, whose belief in me, and his action in championing both me and my mission, means so much. I'm so very grateful. There are so many others I could mention, but I'd hate to miss someone, so please know how deeply I appreciate you all. Your support means the world, and I only hope to pay it forward one day.

Men I Have Loved – you have shaped me in ways I could never have anticipated. Through love, loss, connection, and even heartbreak, you have shown me the depth of what it means to be a man in a world that so often asks you to be anything but yourself. You have taught me how to listen beyond words, to see beyond armour, and to understand the silent battles you fight. This book exists because of you. Thank you for the lessons, the love, and the pieces of yourselves you shared with me.

To You, the Reader – thank you for picking up this book, for your curiosity, and for your willingness to explore yourself in ways many never dare to. This journey is yours, and I hope these pages offer you reflection, reassurance, and the insight to step into the life you truly want. Whatever brought you here, I see you. I hear you. I'm rooting for you.

REFERENCES

Page 22 – Science Magazine, Timothy Wilson, https://www.science.org/doi/epdf/10.1126/science.1250830

Page 25 – Office for National Statistics, https://www.ons.gov.uk/peoplepopulationandcommunity/birthsdeathsandmarriages/deaths/bulletins/suicidesintheunitedkingdom/2023

Page 25 – Centers for Disease, Control and Prevention https://www.cdc.gov/nchs/products/databriefs/db509.htm

Page 138 – How to Do the Work: Recognize Your Patterns, Heal from Your Past, and Create Your Self – Dr. Nicole LePera (Orion Spring, 2021)

Page 139 – When the Body Says No: The Cost of Hidden Stress – Dr. Gabor Maté (Vermilion, 2019)

Page 140 – The Body Keeps the Score: Brain, Mind, and Body in the Healing of Trauma – Bessel van der Kolk (Penguin, 2015)

Page 181 – In the Realm of Hungry Ghosts: Close Encounters with Addiction – Dr. Gabor Maté (Vermilion, 2018)

Page 213 – Attached: The New Science of Adult Attachment and How It Can Help You Find and Keep Love – Dr. Amir Levine & Rachel S.F. Heller (Bluebird, 2011)

Page 219 – The Seven Principles for Making Marriage Work, John Gottman, Ph.D and Nan Silver (Orion Spring, 2018)

STAY CONNECTED

This book is just the beginning of the conversation. If something in these pages resonated with you, I'd love to stay in touch. Whether you're exploring new perspectives, redefining success, or simply curious about what's next, there are ways to keep the momentum going.

JOIN MY NEWSLETTER

Be the first to receive insights, resources, and updates, straight to your inbox. Twice a month, I share reflections, book recommendations, and practical tools to help you navigate the journey of unlearning and rediscovery. Sign up at www.cassandraandrews.com/newsletter

CONNECT ON LINKEDIN

Let's continue the conversation. I regularly share thoughts, articles, and discussions on masculinity, success, and personal growth. Follow and connect with me on linkedin.com/in/cassandraandrews

VISIT MY WEBSITE

Explore more resources, coaching insights, and ways to work together at www.cassandraandrews.com.

If this book spoke to you, reach out – I'd love to hear your thoughts.